How to Improve Study Habits

Four Windows Press

2020

Sturgeon Bay, WI

For more Tips to Starting College, visit:

www.tipstostartingcollege.com

Do you have a job interview coming up? Are you unsure about the process? Get this simple, easy to read job interview guide that will help you gain more confidence to land the job!

Purchase it on Amazon.

Table of Contents

INTRODUCTION

Too many students' grades are falling, especially in a time when regular classrooms cannot fully open. Parents everywhere are at a loss regarding what to do with their responsibilities in the face of the increasing downturn in their children's grades. It seems as though, with the advent of social media, the attention of a lot of students has been shifted from their books to their smartphones or computers. Apart from social media, blame has also been put on a decline in the interest of students regarding education in general. Students, at the moment, do not have the motivation or zeal, as it seems, to even study.

In the last decade there has been a steady decline in the level of interest exhibited by young people regarding their academics, which has translated to the low grades experienced. However, the tip for solving the problem is one that has been followed for decades: discipline. More importantly, discipline to develop good study habits.

Good study habits, or skills, are solutions to the problems experienced by students. This has been true for a long time, but the world is changing rapidly, which also means that the tools employed during study have to be changed in order to keep up.

This is especially true as a result of the covid-19 pandemic that has forced students to study and learn from home rather than in the classroom. E-Learning, or online learning, can be effective, but only if the student has the discipline and drive to succeed using the tools and materials they are provided by teachers. Without strong study skills the student will fall behind in the classroom. Online the failure to develop good study skills can be devastating, leading to an inability to achieve the success in life the student could otherwise achieve.

Developing and maintaining good study habits and skills is no easy task. But it is the way to go. The student, for instance, needs to learn to divide study time by all of the courses they are taking and not only the ones they prefer. They also need to learn to develop a specific regimen and be consistent.

It may be that the student has a set pattern they are following during study sessions. Nevertheless, if there are still deficits with excellent grades despite the skills being utilized, then there is definitely something wrong with the student's study plan.

The purpose of this book is not only to demonstrate with clear examples the types of study habits, but also to show the specific skills students need in order to excel. The expectation is that if the advice is followed in this book, the student will have mastered great study skills.

CHAPTER ONE

Understanding Study Skills

Study skills are the practices implemented by a student during study. Simply put, there are skills and habits which a student, or a person, employs while studying in order to make the most out of the experience. The kind of skills employed by a person, whether good or bad, determines how successful they will be in the process of learning.

Mastering good study habits and study skills inevitably leads to success. This is an important lesson to learn. Good grades cannot be achieved without studying. Having good study skills helps one to study well. By this same logic, students who have mastered good study habits will naturally make better grades. As they advance in school, the stakes become higher and the level of tasks they are expected to complete also becomes more difficult. Only the ones that have mastered great study skills can maximize success.

However, the focus should not be on just making sure the student makes great grades. That is part of a successful college experience, but more importantly, the goal is to help the person become a better student so that they will have good study habits in every field.

Eventually, when the student begins to work in a multimillion dollar industry and is required to study and research large volumes of data and interpret them, or write reports or memos based upon what they have learned on the job, they will not have difficulty because the skill to achieve that will come naturally to them.

Having great study skills does wonders for a student's psyche and confidence. As already pointed out, excellent study skills help to maintain good grades, and good grades have a way of not only enhancing the student's persona, but also improving their level of confidence. Confidence is important. A student with low self-esteem will find it difficult to interact with fellow classmates and instructors, which may actively impact their academic performance.

Great study habits also means that the student will experience less stress and anxiety related to exams. Often examinations are taken with the threat of failure hanging over a student's head. This is usually the case when a student is not prepared. The fear of failure often brings with it anxiety. Students who face anxiety caused by the fear of failure may find it difficult to concentrate. This failure may even result in an inability to maintain relationships, which can spiral into depression. Students who suffer anxiety in the face of examinations can end up eventually failing, which further pushes them into depression. Each of these situations can be prevented by the development and implementation of strong study skills.

Sadly, there are no shortcuts to success. If you are experiencing anxiety tied to your academics, the best thing you can do is look for ways to improve your grades. When grades rise, the spirit of the person will also rise, and anxiety will decrease.

Finally, good study skills may allow the student to have more free time to engage in other activities. A skill a student ought to learn is time management. The process of learning how to manage time effectively will help divide your time. Students who do not practice study skills often find they do not have enough time to engage in all their desired every day activities. When you have good study skills, by extension, you will also have the ability to manage your time, which will free you to engage in other activities while being academically successful.

Study skills are quite different from study techniques. People often make the mistake of thinking they are the same thing. Study skills are the precursor to study techniques. After you have mastered study skills you can move on to learning good study techniques and how to apply them to your everyday study. If you are a student struggling with your academics, the first logical step is to get a firm grasp of study skills. If you begin to learn study techniques without first understanding study skills, implementing those techniques will be difficult because study skills help to prepare you to apply study techniques.

Types of Study Skills

1. Notetaking

Many people fail to take notes because they believe that notetaking is either a waste of their time or that they will remember what they need to know when put to the test. Unfortunately, remembering does not always work out that way.

The main reason we forget is that there is always more information to process than we expect. When you leave the classroom you may immediately encounter fresh information that you then have to store through the same process you used to store the earlier information. If a friend expresses anger at you, or some other personal gossip or conflict or relationship is going on, that may seem more important than what you were sure you would remember, and then there is the information from other classes or reading or a conversation with an instructor. Therefore, you will most likely forget the earlier information because of the pileup of new information you have received. Sometimes the information can get confused in your brain. Taking notes is the best way to ensure you won't lose the information you are trying to store.

However, more important than just taking notes is taking notes properly. Effective notetaking strategies need to be employed if you want to make sure your notetaking helps you when you take a test or write a paper.

Several notetaking strategies can be employed, but the most important point is that you need to understand what strategy works best for you. For some people, in order for them to take notes properly, have to process what they hear and then break it down using their own words. Others prefer the use of diagrams and illustrations. These strategies will be discussed in greater detail a little later in the book. The important thing is to determine what works for you and then incorporate that into your practice of notetaking.

2. Flashcards

Flashcards are visual cues on paper. They are usually cut-out cards with specific information written on them, which helps a person learn and memorize facts or a concept. There are already-made flashcards on various subjects. For instance, a lot of elementary school students have flashcards for learning vocabulary or the times tables.

However, a person can decide to make flashcards for themselves, taking into consideration how they want them to look or how they want to use them. Flashcards work because of how small they are. A student can simply rearrange the cards to their preference, and, in the instance a fact, idea, or concept is forgotten, a card can be picked out of the pile, and the memorization process can be continued. Flashcards can also be picked at random, thus enabling the student to review different areas of a particular subject, repeating what they are trying to memorize until it is firmly in their memory. There are also online flashcard study tools such as *Quizlet, Flashcard Machine, Study Blue, Study Stack*, and *Cram* that have been developed to mimic the functions of flashcards. An Internet search can lead you to each of these study tools.

3. Rehearsing

Rehearsing is also known as memorization. It is the process of storing information in your memory to be recalled later. It is a slow and deliberate process that involves reviewing of information several times to make sure that it has been stored in the memory. Memorization is very important, and students need to discover the discipline and concentration to learn how to memorize material.

Usually, the information that you want to memorize is data, or ideas, that you will need to recall in the future. This information might be for an examination, or just something random, such as phone numbers or house addresses. For students taking examinations, memorization is an indispensable tool that allows you to excel and get good grades.

Also, there are times when you need to memorize facts in order to write complex papers or prepare for interviews when looking through multiple books or materials which may not make a lot of sense at the time.

The most important aspect of memorization is the repetition of what needs to be memorized. Speaking out loud, listening to repetitive audio, repetition works best because you make use of two sensory organs, the ears and the mouth, while repeating what you are trying to memorize. Rehearsal may also include reading a passage or literature many times over and over, in order to become familiar with the subject matter so that you have the ability to recall it easily.

4. Diagrams

Many students are more likely to remember a picture than a written article. The same can be said for what has been visualized using the mind's eye. A smart study skill is to reduce everything to a diagram. There are some techniques that make use of visual skills, such as the *Loci Method*. This technique reduces every piece of information to an actual physical location. As the information comes in, it is immediately associated with a familiar physical location, such as your home, a friend's home or extended family, which helps with the retention of such information.

Diagrams are quite useful because they can be used in several ways. They can be used on their own while studying, which works very well, especially if the student makes the diagram themselves. Even more effective is when the diagram is created during notetaking in class. The student gets to associate the diagram with the information shared during the tutoring process, which can help you remember the information for a longer period of time. Additionally, diagrams can be converted to flashcards and used for studying. It has already been pointed out how effective flashcards can be; therefore, combining flashcards and diagrams is often very useful.

Apart from the general rule that most people retain information when it is conveyed using pictures, some individual's primary method of learning is through the use of visual aids. Many people often find that is extremely difficult to retain information through any other means.

5. Reading

Reading is left for last because it is the most important of all the study skills. It is also the most basic. If a person masters the process of reading, they will be halfway through the process of learning the various study skills. Reading, apart from listening, is the primary process of receiving information that is supposed to be stored in a person's mind.

Reading also helps with critical thinking. When the student reads, they can analyze what they have read with what they understand the topic to be in order to come to a conclusion regarding the subject. One of the techniques used to make this possible is the *REAP* system. *REAP* is an acronym that stands for Read, Encode, Annotate, and Ponder.

Read simply stands for reading the passage to get the idea being passed to the reader by the author. To *Encode* means to paraphrase and rearrange the subject using the student's own words. This helps to make the author's perspective clearer to the student. When the student paraphrases a passage in their own words, it no longer seems abstract, which makes it easier to understand. To *Annotate* means to make notes, usually on the margins of the text. The notes are supposed to explain what is understood about the passage, or to identify any confusion about the passage. This allows the student to find what they need to get back to if the note is either about the importance of the passage being read or a passage that needs to be better understood. To *Ponder* is to go over what was read. Thinking, or pondering, about an idea or information makes things clearer. Oftentimes, it is during the time of pondering and rehearsing that the student finally grasps the full extent of what is being read.

Another reading technique is the *PQRST* method. *PQRST* stands for Preview, Question, Read, Summary, and Test. The method is primarily used to fashion reading in such a way that the student bears in mind that the intention is to answer questions. This method is typically advised for students who are preparing for examinations.

In the *Preview* stage the student reviews the subject matter of what is to be read in order to get a broad outline of it. At the *Question* stage the student formulates questions that ought to be answered at the end of the reading. It is important to conduct the *Preview* before the formulation of the questions so that the student can have a fair idea of what they are going to be asked. Next is the *Reading* stage. While reading the student pays more attention to the areas that provide answers to the questions already formulated. As stated earlier, the *PQRST* method works to provide a focus on certain key areas. At the *Summary* stage, the student tries to discuss the whole subject matter using their own words. Last is the *Test* stage, which the student's analyzation of which questions were covered and answered.

HOW DO YOU READ WHILE STUDYING?

1. I browse the headings, pictures, charts, questions, and summaries before I start reading a chapter:
   - o Never or Rarely
   - o Sometimes
   - o Usually
   - o Always

2. I make questions from a chapter before, during, and after reading it:
   - o Never or Rarely

- o Sometimes
- o Usually
- o Always

3. When reading a unit of material, I summarize it in my own words:
   - o Never or Rarely
   - o Sometimes
   - o Usually
   - o Always

4. I look up information and words that I don't understand:
   - o Never or Rarely
   - o Sometimes
   - o Usually
   - o Always

5. I look for the main ideas as I read:
   - o Never or Rarely
   - o Sometimes
   - o Usually
   - o Always

CHAPTER TWO

Types of Learners

The preceding chapter mentioned that some people are auditory learners. There are also visual learners, kinesthetic learners, and even learners that learn best by reading. The differences stem from the fact that we all experience the world differently. Thus, the different ways we receive, retain, and use information also differs.

Learning about the different types of learning methods is important because it helps educators know how to cater to the needs of every student in their class. It can also eliminate some students lagging behind simply because the mode of teaching in the class is not best for them.

As a student, finding the type of learning style best suited for you is essential because it helps you know what works for you and what doesn't. The process of self-realization will eliminate many problems and help you focus your attention on the actual skills needed to excel academically. For instance, if you are an auditory learner, you will prioritize listening in class by taking notes. During your study time, it would be wise as an auditory learner, to listen to recordings, if the recordings are available, instead of reading. If auditory tapes are not available you will still have to read.

Scientists have continuously researched the steps to be carried out for each learning style. One of the models developed by scientists is the

VARK method. *VARK* stands for Visual, Auditory, Reading, and Kinesthetic. The *VARK* method focuses on just the four prominent types of learners. After learning about all four you will take a quiz to determine what type of learner you are:

1. Visual Learners

A visual learner does better with graphics than with written information. Typically, you will find that a visual learner will prefer to learn by using a graph or diagram. For instance, a visual learner will want to have a feel for the action. So, if an experiment is being conducted, they will want to be present to observe everything from start to finish. As a result, the information is stored longer in their memory. Visual learning is also called spatial learning.

If you are a visual learner you should look for ways to reduce everything to a graphic form. If a board is used during instruction, your eyes should be focused on the board the entire time. Furthermore, make sure that you take notes, even if you end up just making doodles. You will be more comfortable seeing the information written down in your own handwriting.

As a visual learner you may need more time to process the information. This is because you need to process the visual cues you receive to stay focused. There will be no time to slack off. At the end of each class you need to review what you have written down to ensure that your notes are clear. Also, if there are diagrams or flyers, reviewing them immediately after a class will be beneficial.

Visual Learner Example

Sarah loved being at the front of the class. She felt like it was the only place she could actually learn. From there she could see the board and observe demonstrations clearly without obstructions. One time she sat at the back of the room and felt like she was lost the entire period. When taking notes, she would often use graphs, diagrams, and colors to help her remember the information. Sarah struggled in lectures to retain the information being presented despite her best efforts. Because of that her grades in lecture heavy classes weren't great. Sarah started to think that she just wasn't good in those subjects.

Sarah is a visual learner. She needs to keep that in mind when studying a new subject. If the class is going to be lecture heavy, then she needs to focus harder on what is being said and write down important information. She could also record the lecture if the teacher will allow that and transcribe it at a later time. She can put her notes in different visual mediums. Using colors to highlight important facts, converting information into charts and graphs, even doodling a picture that corresponds with the information can be useful. Sarah could also use the Internet to find videos on the subject that present the information in a more visual way. Anything that keeps her visually engaged will be an asset.

2. Kinesthetic Learners

Kinesthetic learners are also known as experiential or tactile learners. They learn best from experiencing, or actually "doing," instead of just being told something or watching a demonstration. Kinesthetic learners also like to act things out. If an experience is being shared, a kinesthetic learner will learn best by being part of the illustration given in that situation. If you are good at dancing or playing sports, you may be a kinesthetic learner. Kinesthetic learners should use study techniques such as flashcards to turn simple recall into a game, studying in short blocks that help with a short attention span, using plenty of examples when writing study notes. Studying with other people and talking about what you've learned is often a great way to consolidate what you are trying to learn. Doing something actionable while you study such as tapping a pencil or squeezing a stress ball and listening to music while studying tends to be less distracting for kinesthetic learners while studying than it is for other people.

Kinesthetic Learners Example

Ayla has a hard time not moving around and making noise during class. Her hands are constantly moving, whether it's tapping her fingers or clicking a pen. She often is scolded for her inability to sit still. She loves being given projects to do. Ayla always gets excellent grades on projects, but when it comes to classwork she barely passes. Class is boring to her, and she feels disconnected from the rest of the class. She finds it very difficult to stay focused in class, and it hinders her ability to learn. Ayla doesn't understand why she is doing so poorly. Ayla excels in sports and has played competitively in different sports. She can pick up a new sport very easily.

Ayla is a kinesthetic learner. She needs to be hands-on with the things she learns. She needs to adapt techniques that can help her stay focused. In class she should find quieter ways to channel her need to move, like squeezing a stress ball or doodling. At home she can try pacing as she reads. Ayla should also break-up her study time into multiple smaller parts instead of studying during a single long block of time. Making flashcards or turning study materials into a game would be beneficial. Kinesthetic learners are also easily overwhelmed, so learning relaxation techniques can help combat that.

3. Auditory Learners

Auditory learners are apt to learn more if the subject is amplified using sounds. An auditory learner will prefer spending hours listening to a lecture as opposed to actually reading the text. This is because they tend to remember what they hear more than what they read. Auditory learners may also be good at explaining complex material to others.

If you discover that you are an auditory learner, then you need to make sure you attend all of the lectures. You may want to record the lectures and ask a fellow student to record a missed lecture so you can listen to it later. Alternatively, you could also read out-loud to yourself. The important thing is to listen to the sound of what is being read. Which means you will tend to remember and retain more.

Auditory learners can also learn with the aid of music. Apart from the fact that music can calm you down, the music can also help you become receptive to new knowledge. It can also be a tool for learning in itself.

Auditory Learners Example

Elijah excels in his social studies and language arts classes, but when it comes to math and science, he just can't seem to retain the information. It's almost like math and science are in a different universe than the one where he lives. Elijah tries his best and asks questions in class all the time. Despite that he still struggles to understand certain topics. Elijah has also found he is gifted at learning languages, especially from recordings. He has, in the past, been bullied for mouthing the words as he reads books. Now Elijah mostly uses audiobooks and has a much easier time retaining what the book says. Elijah has noticed that when the classroom is intense he has a hard time focusing, like his brain wants to listen to everything that is going on all at once.

Elijah is an auditory learner. He learns best by listening to information. Elijah can adjust his study habit to best utilize his skills. Recording lectures to listen to later is a great way to help retain the information. During class, he should sit near the front of the room and participate in classroom discussions. Another thing Elijah can do is record himself reading key terms and their definitions and then listen to what he has recorded when he is doing other things, like exercising or walking to school. He can also read assignments out-loud and repeat information to himself with his eyes closed. He can even possibly find audio versions of his textbooks.

4. Reading Learners

Reading learners understand better when they read written text. In some ways there is a connection between reading learners and visual learners. This stems from the fact that both types of learners have to actually visually see what they are trying to learn in order to assimilate it better.

Reading Learners Example

Rowan loves to read and has always had very high reading comprehension. When Rowan digs into a new subject, he gathers all the reading materials he can on the subject. Rowan excels on essays and loves to do research. Lecture heavy subjects are harder for Rowan to grasp, and he often has to look up other resources to help understand them. Rowan also likes to handwrite his notes, whereas other students prefer to type their notes. Rowan usually rewrites his notes to make them clearer and easier to read. He also annotates them with extra information he has found in his own reading. Rowan likes to research topics on his own and regularly is at the library, searching for material to help his research.

Rowan is a reading learner. Reading learners are comparable to visual learners, but reading learners rely more heavily on reading and writing to grasp concepts. Rowan would benefit most from getting transcripts of lectures and other medias so that they can be read. Notetaking is highly beneficial for this type of learner, especially rewriting notes to clarify parts that require it. Writing summaries after reading long blocks of text can aid in retention. Unlike visual learners, reading learners do not benefit from charts and graphs. So, Rowan should turn charts and graphs into words. Rowan would also benefit from PowerPoints that are mostly text. Repeatedly writing study materials can also help with retention of information.

There are also lesser known classifications besides the big four discussed above. There are *solitary learners* who are usually fiercely independent and like being on their own. A *solitary learner* will learn best without interference from others. They are typically the students who prefer personal study to classroom study. If you are a *solitary learner*, then you are most likely comfortable with your own thoughts, so you may also like to keep journals, be alone, and enjoy doing self-analysis. As a solitary learner you are best served when you take the materials for study and study on your own, without the interference that being in a room with others may bring.

Social learners are the direct opposite of *solitary learners*. They prefer studying in groups, being in classes, and brainstorming. What they study usually comes easily to them when they have brainstorming sessions with others. If you are a *social learner* then you have to create time to brainstorm when you are done with your personal reading.

Finally, there are *logical learners*. Typically, these sets of individuals learn by asking a lot of questions. The more questions they ask, the more insight they gain into the subject matter, and the better knowledge they acquire of the material being studied. *Logical learners* tend to want to get the full picture and all of the answers. They are usually uncomfortable with incomplete information. If you are a *logical learner*, you would want information laid out to you comprehensively. You will also typically want to categorize everything into compartments. As a *logical learner* you must not be afraid to ask questions. Always procure as much information about the subject matter as you can and try to avoid teachers or tutors who shut you down when you want to ask a question. That sort of relationship has a way of interfering with your psyche and might make you afraid of asking questions in the future. While this may not pose a problem for some people, as a *logical learner* it may be problematic for you because you will be unable to process the information.

Conclusion

Learning about your learning style can be very helpful. It can give you insight into how you approach classes and master the information and knowledge you need for tests and writing papers. However, one note of caution is this, many learners may have more than a single learning style. They may be strong at a reading learning style, for instance, but can also function adequately, if not quite as well, in a lecture-heavy class. Therefore all learners should try to discover their learning style strengths and understand how they can use those strengths to improve their study skills.

WHAT IS YOUR LEARNING STYLE?

There are many different learning styles, and each of us perceives and absorbs information differently. Find out what learning style best suits you! You might be surprised.

Scoring:

A = 1 Point

B = 2 Point

C = 3 Point

D = 4 Point

Total the points together to determine your learning style.

---

1. When I spell, I verify accuracy by:

    a. Looking at the word to see if it looks correct

    b. Sounding the word out in my head

    c. Getting a feeling about the correctness of the spelling

    d. Reading/Writing the word

2. When you study for a test, would you rather:

    a. Look at diagrams and illustrations

    b. Have someone ask you questions

    c. Make models or diagrams yourself

    d. Read notes or write on a notepad

3. What is most distracting for you when you are trying to concentrate?

    a. TV advertisement

    b. Noises

    c. Hunger

    d. Pen with no ink

4. I remember people by:

    a. Names

    b. Faces

    c. The first time I met them

    d. Their message or letter

5. What kind of restaurant would you not like to go in?

    a. Restaurant with fancy bright lights

b. Restaurant with loud music

c. Restaurant with uncomfortable chairs

d. Restaurant with a boring menu card

6. Would you rather go to a/an?

   a. Art Museum

   b. Music Concert

   c. Gym

   d. Crossword Puzzle competition

7. When you see the word "Pizza", what do you do first?

   a. Imagine a cheesy pizza

   b. Say the word "pizza"

   c. Feel the taste of pizza

   d. Read the spellings separately

8. To remember the list of items, I:

   a. Imagine the items in my mind

   b. Repeat the items over and over again

   c. Move my fingers to remember each name

   d. Read the items from the list

9. What will you do if someone is asking you for an address?

   a. Imagine the place and let them know

   b. Speak the exact address loudly and clearly

   c. Take the person with you

   d. Write the address on a piece of paper

10. What is your part in a group project?

    a. Drawing charts and graphs for the plan layout

    b. Give roles to others by speaking

    c. Do whatever the group leader assigns

    d. Write the end documentation

11. In my free time, I like to:

    a. Watch a movie

    b. Listen to music

    c. Draw something

    d. Read a book

12. I like teachers who:

    a. Teach through graphs and charts

    b. Teach through lectures

    c. Teach by giving activities

    d. Teach by letting students read the course

13. What do you do when you are angry?

    a. Make a "mad" face to let people know

    b. Scream and shout

    c. Break everything

    d. Read articles about calming yourself

14. What do you do when you are happy?

    a. Smile

    b. Talk to people

c. Act really hyper

d. Read positive blogs

15. Lastly, what is your favorite subject?

a. Art

b. History

c. Science

d. English

RESULTS:

SCORE RANGE	LEARNING STYLE
0 -15	VISUAL LEARNER
16 - 30	AUDITORY LEARNER
31 - 45	KINESTHETIC LEARNER
46 - 60	READ/WRITE LEARNER

DETAILS:

VISUAL LEARNER:

- Process data using charts & graphs
- Need pictures to clarify concepts
- Prefer graphic elements over words

AUDITORY LEARNER:

- Learn greatest when information is vocal
- Prefer conversations & lectures

- Process information by speaking through things

KINESTHETIC LEARNER:

- Learn best through a tactile process
- Prefer to generate concrete personal experience
- Process information by rehearsal and experimenting

READ/WRITE LEARNER:

- Prefer to receive written words
- Enjoy reading and writing assignments
- Process information by writing notes and key points

How did you do? Were you surprised?

CHAPTER THREE

Developing Great Study Skills

Before you begin to work on your study skills, you need to set goals for yourself. Ask yourself what you want to achieve at the end of the process you are going to use to end up with good study skills. Writing the goals down and displaying them will help you be more definitive about what you are trying to achieve, and it will also help you keep track of the goals.

Your goals should be realistic. Analyze how you have studied in the past and what you have achieved through the way you have studied. Use that as a yardstick to set goals. Grandiose plans are great, but making them may be foolish, especially if you do not have the foundation to achieve good results. Also, you should consider the study skills required to achieve the level of success set by your desired goals compared to the studying style you have employed in the past. This will help you to gain perspective.

Example

Jonah was not good at sitting in class. He has so much energy he has to fight with himself to sit still and listen to his instructors. However, he was so smart he was scary. When he really wanted to learn things, he would grab a book or dig into the Internet and absolutely master what he wanted to learn, seemingly without effort. Still, his grades were not the best by any measure. Instructors expect students to listen, and when he started displaying what he actually did know in a paper, they always suspected he was cheating somehow even if they couldn't figure out how. This was especially true since he either spouted off in class or kept his mouth shut in an effort to keep out of trouble.

Jonah was obviously an independent learner. He needed to understand that and put some effort into making sure he disciplined himself in class, taking notes, doing diagrams, or otherwise keeping his mind on what was being taught. You don't need to be poor at learning to need study skills. Sometimes you need the discipline to force yourself to concentrate. Jonah probably has the brains to get a doctoral degree, but if he is to get through his high school and undergraduate work, he also needs to use good study skill techniques to discipline himself in ways that helps instructors understand just how smart he really is.

1. Know what works for you

Knowing what works for you is the first and most crucial step in developing good study habits. You need to discover what studying style works best for you. This will, in turn, help you determine which studying skills are beneficial to you so that you do not waste your time working on skills that do not achieve maximum results.

The different learning styles have already been discussed. After taking the quiz at the end of Chapter Two, you should know what learning style works best for you. The visual, auditory, kinesthetic and verbal learners all have different methods that work uniquely for them. The type of learner you are will determine such things as the rate at which you study, where you study, and even whether you study with people or on your own.

Example

Cara recently took the quiz to determine what type of learner she was. She found that she scored higher in visual learning with kinesthetic being her second highest. She sat down and looked up what best study tips for those two learning styles were. She found that making her notes more visually appealing would be useful. Color coding and drawing pictures can help make the information easier to understand. She also found that she needed to take lots of breaks so that she could move around, as sitting still for a long time is difficult for her.

Cara hated studying for her history class because it was boring to her. There did not seem to be a lot of things she could do to make the information more fun to look at. She knew that she had to find a better way to study the content because she would often put it off to the last minute, which is stressful. She thought that maybe if she turned it into more of a game and studied with her friends it would be easier. That helped a lot. She ended up making it like a quiz game show. Since then she has stopped putting her studying off and started doing better in class.

Cara setup her desk against a wall so she wouldn't be distracted by things going on outside of her study area. She also kept clutter to a minimum. She managed to procure a comfy desk chair from a garage sale to make sitting at her desk easier. Cara tries to study at the same time every day because she heard that having a routine would help the brain get used to studying at that time. She also read that she should start absorbing information faster if she set up a regular study routine. She mostly studies right after school and tries to set up her study groups for the same time. It seems to work for her.

2. Develop the right mental attitude

Sadly, a lot of students view studying as a chore that needs to be completed as soon (or as close to the last minute) as possible, so they usually designate as little time as possible to the task. However, that is not acceptable if you aim to become a successful student, and, in the end, successful in life. Developing the right mental attitude towards the task of studying is the first step you need to take to be successful.

No matter how much you dislike studying, or how much you dislike studying a particular subject, you should try to find a way to enjoy the experience. Learning to not view studying as unpleasant is also important.

When you begin studying, remove every distraction from your mind and focus on the positive benefits that come from studying. Do not allow emotions to influence study time. If you have any unresolved issues, you should take care of them before you begin studying.

Example

Steven is currently learning French and is struggling slightly. He first thought his trouble had something to do with how he took notes, and he decided to change how he took notes. Steven learned how to write in shorthand and started making his first draft of notes that way.

Later, when he got home, he would rewrite them and organize them in a way that made sense to him. He would make flash cards of the new words he learned that day. It greatly improved his understanding.

Steven also decided to change how he would study words. He found that if he turned his vocabulary lists into a game, he could remember them easier. Steven also joined a study group to help with his conversational skills. The group met once a week. It was the goal during study time to use as little English as possible. It certainly helped that the group was led by someone already fluent in French and could help with grammar and pronunciation. Steven found that his grades skyrocketed after joining the study group. His fluency also greatly improved.

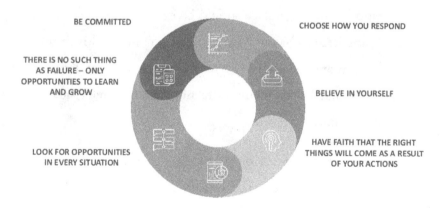

DEVELOPING THE RIGHT MENTAL ATTITUDE

BE COMMITTED

CHOOSE HOW YOU RESPOND

THERE IS NO SUCH THING AS FAILURE – ONLY OPPORTUNITIES TO LEARN AND GROW

BELIEVE IN YOURSELF

LOOK FOR OPPORTUNITIES IN EVERY SITUATION

HAVE FAITH THAT THE RIGHT THINGS WILL COME AS A RESULT OF YOUR ACTIONS

3. Create a study place

There is no limit to the number of places you can study. As a matter of fact, people have studied in unconventional places and managed to be successful. There is something to be said about choosing a specific place to be the location where you study, if not all the time, at least most of the time. In the first place, finding a study place increases predictability. Humans are creatures of habit, and we find ourselves reverting to the habits we have engaged in the past. This, in its own way, enhances our productivity. We begin to associate certain locations with specific activities and thus find it easier to carry out those activities at those locations. For instance, you easily fall asleep on your bed because your brain has come to associate that location with sleep. In the same way, if you designate a particular place as your study area, you will probably find studying easier at that location. Your assimilation rate will also be very high because of the ease with which the study comes to you.

Designating a location as your study area is not difficult. The main consideration is that the place should be comfortable, insulated from noise and interference, as well as relatively secluded. This means that an ideal study area is probably not the couch in your living room because there may be too many distractions with the television turned on and people moving about.

Once you have decided on a place to be your studying/reading location, you need to take steps to ensure that it is comfortable, which may include getting chairs, pillows, and other necessary items that will make you feel comfortable. To avoid distractions you should also consider removing gadgets that will distract you, such as phones and TV.

Equally as important as designating a place to be your study area is designating a study time. As pointed out earlier, the brain gets used to routines, so once you begin reading at a particular period, your brain gets used to that and starts assimilating knowledge or information faster during that period. However, before you choose to start reading at any time, make sure that you have decided the best time for you to be studying. You have to experiment with reading at various times in the day to get used to the time that suits you best. Some individuals find their brains function at its peak early in the morning before they set out for the day's business. For others the middle of the night works best. While you experiment with different times, you have to take into consideration the nature of what you do as well as about how busy your day is. If you have a job or have a habit of getting together with friends right after lunch, that's probably not a good time to choose to study. Choosing a workable time period will go a long way in determining the time most suitable for you.

CREATING A STUDY PLACE

1. I have the "study-place habit" that is, being at a certain place at a certain time means time to study.

    o   Never or Rarely

    o   Sometimes

    o   Usually

    o   Always

2. I try to study during my personal peak energy time to increase my concentration level.

    o   Never or Rarely

- o Sometimes
- o Usually
- o Always

3. I am confident with my level of concentration I am able to maintain.
   - o Never or Rarely
   - o Sometimes
   - o Usually
   - o Always

4. I quiz myself over material that could appear on future quizzes and exams.
   - o Never or Rarely
   - o Sometimes
   - o Usually
   - o Always

5. I practice the materials I am learning by reciting information out loud.
   - o Never or Rarely
   - o Sometimes
   - o Usually
   - o Always

6. I summarize my notes into my own words for better understanding.
   - o Never or Rarely

o Sometimes

o Usually

o Always

7. I try to create associations between my new material I am trying to learn and information I already know.

o Never or Rarely

o Sometimes

o Usually

o Always

8. I recall readily those things which I have studied.

o Never or Rarely

o Sometimes

o Usually

o Always

4. Take great notes

As already pointed out notetaking is an indispensable tool for any student. Remember to take notes to help you keep track of what is being said in class because you may not be able to remember everything that was said, and even when you do manage to remember, your brain may fail to remember what was presented exactly as it was delivered. The only way to make sure you preserve the substance of what is being taught is by either recording the sessions or by taking notes. Also, notes give you something to fall back on when you want to write a paper, take a test, or do revisions in a presentation you are assigned.

When taking notes, only bother with the things you feel are relevant. A lot of things the lecturer might say may not be relevant to the course work, a test, or writing a paper. Your duty is to sieve through all that is said to focus on relevant points and then write. When taking notes the kind of learner you are is also very important. If you are an audio learner making recordings might be the best strategy. If you are a visual learner you can make diagrams as you take notes so that you will find it easier to remember what the lecturer said during your studying period.

Make a habit of reviewing your notes as soon as you can. You should also quickly skim through the notes you made in class. Before you begin any new notes you should revise your previous notes. These techniques will help you retain information. The goal is to get the information to move from your short-term to your long-term memory.

NOTETAKING

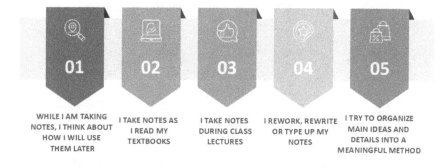

01	02	03	04	05
WHILE I AM TAKING NOTES, I THINK ABOUT HOW I WILL USE THEM LATER	I TAKE NOTES AS I READ MY TEXTBOOKS	I TAKE NOTES DURING CLASS LECTURES	I REWORK, REWRITE OR TYPE UP MY NOTES	I TRY TO ORGANIZE MAIN IDEAS AND DETAILS INTO A MEANINGFUL METHOD

5. Use Memory games

Memory games, also called mnemonics, are methods that can be employed to help you learn and retain information. There are several forms of mnemonics. One example is where keywords from what you need to learn are strung together to form a sentence, which can then be remembered easily. During tests or examination periods, the information can be remembered easily and then applied.

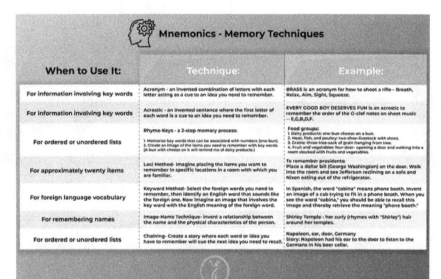

Mnemonics - Memory Techniques

When to Use It:	Technique:	Example:
For information involving key words	Acronym - an invented combination of letters with each letter acting as a cue to an idea you need to remember.	BRASS is an acronym for how to shoot a rifle-- Breath, Relax, Aim, Sight, Squeeze.
For information involving key words	Acrostic - an invented sentence where the first letter of each word is a cue to an idea you need to remember.	EVERY GOOD BOY DESERVES FUN is an acrostic to remember the order of the G-clef notes on sheet music -- E,G,B,D,F.
For ordered or unordered lists	Rhyme-Keys - a 2-step memory process: 1. Memorize key words that can be associated with numbers (one-bun). 2. Create an image of the items you need to remember with key words. (A bun with cheese on it will remind me of dairy products.)	Food groups: 1. Dairy products: one-bun-cheese on a bun. 2. Meat, fish, and poultry: two-shoe-livestock with shoes. 3. Grains: three-tree-sack of grain hanging from tree. 4. Fruit and vegetables: four-door- opening a door and walking into a room stocked with fruits and vegetables.
For approximately twenty items	Loci Method- Imagine placing the items you want to remember in specific locations in a room with which you are familiar.	To remember presidents: Place a dollar bill (George Washington) on the door. Walk into the room and see Jefferson reclining on a sofa and Nixon eating out of the refrigerator.
For foreign language vocabulary	Keyword Method- Select the foreign words you need to remember, then identify an English word that sounds like the foreign one. Now imagine an image that involves the key word with the English meaning of the foreign word.	In Spanish, the word "cabina" means phone booth. Invent an image of a cab trying to fit in a phone booth. When you see the word "cabina," you should be able to recall this image and thereby retrieve the meaning "phone booth."
For remembering names	Image-Name Technique- invent a relationship between the name and the physical characteristics of the person.	Shirley Temple - her curly (rhymes with "Shirley") hair around her temples.
For ordered or unordered lists	Chaining- Create a story where each word or idea you have to remember will cue the next idea you need to recall.	Napoleon, ear, door, Germany Story: Napoleon had his ear to the door to listen to the Germans in his beer cellar.

TIPS TO SURVIVE
COLLEGE

6. Practice with friends

Your friends or fellow students can help you implement a good study strategy. During your studies, if you prefer studying with a group of people, after studying and during the revision stage, your friends can also be of assistance. Brainstorming can be a great way to help you retain information.

You can have a session where you discuss what you have read with friends. The process of reviewing what you have read or simply just saying it out loud can give you insight into areas where you need further help. You can also review past examinations, questions, and tests. Flashcards can be used in order to test the accuracy of your memory and whether you have assimilated what you studied.

You have to consider that while practicing with old examination questions, the pattern of the questions may change. The lecturer may simply change the model of the questions, words them differently, or uses different questions on the same subject altogether, so you need to be cautious while studying. If you have examples from tests given by the instructor for that class in the past. The whole essence of reviewing past questions is to gain insight into possible examination questions. There is no guarantee that those questions will be exactly the same as the questions on a test in the future.

You need to evaluate if studying with other people works for you. Some people are able to study while having friends around during their study or revision periods, while others may not tolerate that. You need to determine what style of studying is most beneficial to you.

CHAPTER FOUR

Improving Your Study Skills

We have discussed the types of good study skills. However, there is a need for continuity. So, how do you use the skills you have learned so that they become a part of you and not just something that you engage in any time you have an examination?

1. Set a trial period

Once you have started practicing good study habits, you need to make them become a part of you, which can only be done through practice. A trial period gives you the opportunity to practice as much as you want and is typically one month or thirty days. An educator by the name of Steve Pavlina popularized the concept of the trial period. According to him, if a habit is practiced for as long as 30 days, it becomes part of the person and cannot easily be shaken.

During the 30-day period you should try and focus on specific study habits. Some of them have been listed previously. You should focus on one at a time for a given period. By doing so, you will have the time to devote to a single habit and avoid distractions.

The trial period should be during a time when you do not have any exams to take, thus, you will not have any pressing incentive to study except the need to improve your study habits. That way, you will find it easier to start and also have the strength to continue if you get bored or discouraged. Furthermore, just reading for the sake of reading helps you to be a more prepared and better student. Waiting for the period of examinations before you begin studying does not work because you will be ill-equipped to handle any impromptu tests that may come up during your classes. You should work with the mindset that an examination, short answer, essay, or multiple choice, could be given at any time, and you may be called upon to write answers to questions as well. So, when you set your trial date, even though you do not have any examinations during that period, you can work as though you are preparing for an examination. Keep in mind that testing could occur at any time and prepare adequately for it.

During your preparations you should know that studying is not easy. As a matter of fact, learning anything new is not easy, and learning the right study skills is no exception. At some point you may become tired and unmotivated. Your responsibility during those times is to maintain your study schedule. You need to find inner motivation. Eventually the practice of studying will get easier, and studying will come more naturally to you. Learning the right study skills is something you should be willing to learn on your own.

Example

Aviva nearly failed last year. She told herself that this year was going to be different. She didn't want the stress of almost failing again. She knew she needed to develop better study habits. She looked up different study techniques over the summer and planned to try them out when school started. She read somewhere that she should only start one at a time. Trying to do more could overwhelm her and make it harder to keep up the good study habits she was developing. So, Aviva resolved to focus on her notetaking for the first month of school. After that she would work on how she reviewed her notes.

Halfway through the year Aviva found it was getting harder to keep up her new habits. She was losing her motivation to keep it up. She knew she needed to find a new way to get motivated because just the desire to get good grades wasn't motivating her anymore. Aviva had to find something more important to motivate her. Aviva sat down and discussed it with her parents, and her dad suggested she focus on learning the material. He suggested that she should invest her time and effort into becoming more knowledgeable. People who were successful usually knew a lot. That seemed like a more worthwhile endeavor for Aviva. She found what motivated her and was able to make the changes throughout the year by using her new study plan.

2. Focus on learning

A good way to improve your reading skills is to focus on learning instead of just reading to pass examinations. For the skills to become a part of you, you need a higher purpose – something that drives you beyond getting good grades. No doubt the quest for excellent grades can act as an excellent motivator, but that only lasts for so long. Furthermore, grades show how much you have covered within a specific time range. Grades can be arbitrary and may not be a perfect tool to discern how much of the subject the individual has actually internalized. Thus, the results from receiving a higher grade or another may be poor and cannot be fully trusted.

When you no longer have any examinations, you may begin to lose motivation. Thus, a stronger reason will be to learn just for the sake of learning. Those people who know a lot as a result of study are usually the most successful people around. Ideally, if you have the right study skills, you may not need to worry about making good grades because that should naturally follow as a matter of course.

Example

Ellis always felt like he didn't have enough time in the day to study. Between school and his part-time job he felt like he was always on the run. He just couldn't figure out how to study with the time constraints he was given, and his grades started to suffer because of it. Ellis was beginning to worry about his grades. A friend of his recommended that Ellis record the lectures in class and listen to them as he walked to and from work and school. The friend also mentioned that he take his flashcards to work with him and quizzes himself on his breaks. Ellis took her advice and realized that he could manage his time better and sneak in a bit of studying where he could. It improved his grades immensely.

Ellis also noticed that he was always feeling sluggish and tired. It made him not want to do anything with the free time he did have to study. Ellis decided to look into ways to feel better. Almost everything he came across said to make sure you were drinking enough water. Being dehydrated makes you feel sluggish. Ellis decided to carry a water bottle and refill it when he could. Within a few days Ellis noticed a big difference in his energy levels. Ellis continued to make sure he carried water with him every day.

One day Ellis' teacher asked them to relate the newest lesson to something in the real world. Ellis looked into it and was able to transfer the skills they were learning to several job descriptions. That inspired Ellis to check and see what other lessons could be transferred into real world skills. Doing so helped Ellis understand the importance of certain lessons. Once he understood how important they were to what he wanted to accomplish in life it was easier to motivate himself to study it.

3. Use your time wisely

One way to continuously improve your study skills is by apportioning your time correctly. You should know that taking your time seriously is one of the best ways to strengthen your study skills.

During lectures you need to learn the peculiarities of your instructors and make sure that you attend all your lectures. You will learn more from some than others. Try to determine why you are not learning as much from that one lecturer and if that is something you can fix. Learning is always up to the individual that wants to learn in the end. A lecturer can give you information, insight, or knowledge, but if you do not take the responsibility to absorb that, then you will not learn.

You also need to understand what mode the lecturer uses in dispensing grades. Some lectures grade students on their attendance to lectures or participation in classes.

TIME MANAGEMENT CHECKLIST

1. I use a planner (or other method) to write down upcoming academic and personal activities.

    o   Never or Rarely

    o   Sometimes

    o   Usually

    o   Always

2. I use a "to do list" to keep track of completing my academic and personal activities

    o   Never or Rarely

o   Sometimes

o   Usually

o   Always

3. I schedule definite times on my calendar for study time.
    o   Never or Rarely
    o   Sometimes
    o   Usually
    o   Always

4. I start studying for quizzes and tests at least several days before I take them.
    o   Never or Rarely
    o   Sometimes
    o   Usually
    o   Always

5. I start papers and projects as soon as they are assigned.
    o   Never or Rarely
    o   Sometimes
    o   Usually
    o   Always

6. I have a system or know how to prioritize my classes and other life activities.
    o   Never or Rarely
    o   Sometimes

o Usually

o Always

7. I have enough time for school and fun.
   o Never or Rarely
   o Sometimes
   o Usually
   o Always

4. Eat well

No matter how much time you give to studying and mastering study skills, if you do not eat properly, the results may be dismal. To keep you going you need to learn to feed your brain with the right nutrients to grow and become stronger. Eating and exercising correctly are important. The nutrients you consume can have a huge impact on your brain and can either speed up your attempt to learn material or slow your attempt down.

When you do not eat healthy foods, as opposed to those times you spend eating junk and other unhealthy food, you are putting a strain on your heart and every other part of your body. This is hardly ideal for studying. You should also make sure you are drinking enough water. Brain cells rely on the amount of water they get, so when your brain is not being hydrated, a lot of problems, such as anxiety, can influence long-term retention.

5. Connect to real life

You need to relate everything you've learned to the real world. Find a way to make what you are studying relevant to your life as an individual, and it will help improve the skills you already possess.

CHAPTER FIVE

Bad Study Habits: How Do I Know Them?

Study habits differ just as students differ. As students grow in their educational pursuit, some study habits they have adopted remain effective, while others are no longer useful and are dropped. You basically study to maintain your academic growth, so the way and manner in which you study reflects the results. If you spend the bulk of your time reading, and you still do not understand the content, or you still under-perform, then you should consider checking your study habits to ensure you have not been adopting bad ones. Below are some of the bad study habits you should try to avoid.

1. Cramming

Cramming information mostly arises from not having prepared well for an exam. Sometimes it arises as a result of bad studying habits that we are not conscious of practicing. Students who do not schedule and maintain consistent times during the day to read and study are not usually prepared. When preparing for a test, students should study and read for 2 or 3 hours every day instead of doing an all-nighter a day before the test or exam. Resting your body and brain before a test or exam is essential to help your body and brain stay healthy. When you cram for a test you strain your brain and you may find that it's difficult to get a good grade.

Example

Terri often spent the night before every test cramming, often pulling all-nighters. She always passes, but just barely. Instead of getting enough rest for her body and mind, she puts others under strain, which makes focusing on her test near impossible, although she will deny that's the case. Another issue Terri has is that she tries to multitask when she does decide to study ahead of time. Splitting her focus between two or three different tasks makes it hard to retain any information. One of the biggest distractions for Terri is music. She often stops focusing on her study materials to sing along or dance to a song she likes. While music can be beneficial for some people, it just distracts Terri.

Due to her poor study habits, Terri sometimes skips classes to catch up or she misses a test she hadn't been able to study for. When she skips class it just puts her more behind. She misses information provided in that class, and she may now have to put in twice as much effort to catch up. In the end skipping class almost always does more harm than good.

2. Multitasking

When it comes to reading, understanding, and passing your exams or tests, multitasking does not usually help you achieve good grades. You should focus when you read. You cannot be engaged in another activity while reading. This drains your time and energy and leaves you unable to focus properly. You are generally less focused when you multitask than when you concentrate on finishing one activity at a time. Research has shown that those constantly checking information on electronic devices have problems focusing and recalling information as they move from one task to the next. On the other hand, persons who merely engage in one activity or task before moving onto the next are more focused and able to recall more information.

Example

Sean was told once that he would have a hard time staying organized due to how smart he was. He was told he would have to work at overcoming his aversion to getting himself organized. He did not heed the advice, nor did he learn how to properly organize. His disorganization was most apparent when he would try to study. His materials were always all over the place, and his desk was cluttered. He didn't take notes in a way that was useful to him. He didn't know how to make an outline. Everything was completely out of order, and studying effectively was a problem.

Like most young adults Sean loves social media. He has a hard time putting his phone down to study. He would start reading a passage and get a notification on his phone. He often picks up his phone and ends up scrolling for five to ten minutes before he gets back to studying.

When studying you need to focus fully on what you are reading, or you won't retain what you have just read. Along with not being able to retain information, Sean ends up spending more time on his phone than studying. This has made his studying ineffectual.

3. Listening to music

Listening to music has been proven to be very useful when studying for a lot of people. This is because the music we listen to has the potential of motivating us to be more active, or at rest, and to think deeply. Music engages your thoughts. However, for some people, listening to music is not beneficial when studying. This is a very personal thing. The reasoning for this is simple: listening to music can engage you and divert your attention and mind from your present state and from your studies. But for other people it may help open their mind, and they can study more effectively. Therefore you need to understand yourself and find out what works best for you.

You need to be honest with yourself too. If you love music, and want to listen to it all of the time, but it interferes with your studying, you have to accept what is happening and make a change. We are all good at justifying ourselves when it comes to doing what we want to do rather than what we should do. Therefore sometimes you need to accept what the problem is and then take action to focus on learning correctly.

4. Skipping classes

The reasons why classes are scheduled are to sharpen your understanding and to help you focus your mind on reading material and preparing for mastering class content. When you skip classes you are likely to spend twice the time it would take a person who attended that class to read and understand the notes and class material. Attending every class and doing so on time requires great discipline and determination, especially in college with little or no surveillance from anyone to ensure class is being attended.

When you are studying online, however, the issue of skipping classes does not come into the picture because you have all the information available, but then you have to keep working at a steady pace, reading and studying, to be able to even complete an online course. One of the major reasons so many students do not complete online courses is that they fail to maintain a schedule of completing work every single day. A great degree of self-motivation is needed to earn good grades.

5. Absence of a proper outline

Your outline for reading should specify the time you would spend reading and what time you need to start. Keeping an outline before you commence your reading helps you organize your ideas and analyze what you need to study, as well as when you should study. This is particularly useful when you have a bulky text to cover. When you do not keep outlines, you may miss the important topics and end up focusing on less important details of a course while devoting little or no time to more crucial subject matter.

6. Using social media while studying

Social media addiction is a great threat to good study habits, and it can keep you from receiving the grades you are working to receive. Social media addiction stems from the fact that we do not want to be left out. From Instagram to Twitter, Facebook and Snapchat, we want to know what the latest gist is about. Setting your priorities to accommodate your studies first is important. To achieve this, try freezing your social media apps, or, alternatively, use an app to set a time when your social media accounts will be inactive to enable you to study. The time fixed should correlate with the time you have scheduled for studying. This requires great discipline and determination, together with constant practice. The aim is to ensure that when you read you are not constantly checking your phone.

7. Not actively studying

Merely reading and taking notes is not enough. While reading, try to fully engage yourself in what you are reading and ensure that you have a good understanding of the content. You should be able to comfortably explain what you have read in your own words. Use some creative study strategies such as giving yourself a quiz or teaching someone what you have learned. Reading and then testing yourself works well in helping your retentiveness because you are tasking yourself to retain information from your memory without referencing a textbook.

8. Being disorganized

There is a lot of information to process and take notes of when you read and study, so being disorganized will not be beneficial. You should take notes and keep reminders in an organized way. Some people are great at taking notes and do so voluminously, but then they have trouble finding what they are looking for when they need to review their notes on specific content.

For every course having a separate notebook for taking notes is very helpful. You should also keep your study schedule posted at a place where you can easily see it. Your notebook containing schedules should be available to record exam dates and keep track of your assignments, deadlines, and study schedules. There are apps available that can help you organize your studies and do all these for you. The only disadvantage is not being able to do anything if your phone is not working or you are unable to access your phone from a particular location.

9. Not having a study space

There are no fixed places for studying, but there are places you should avoid when trying to study. For instance, studying at home can be difficult. There are many distractions at home, such as the TV and family interruptions. You can avoid this by finding a quiet place to study. That place can still be in your home, but not where there can be distractions. You should consider studying at the public library. Ensure that your studying area is quiet and free from distractions.

10. Studying with the wrong people

When you are formulating a study plan you should consider working with a friend or fellow students. Choose people who are also focused on achieving good grades. Choosing the right people to study with is very important. If your friends are as motivated to read as you are, and you are studying together, you can encourage each other. If you get together with your friends to study and you all end up focusing on entirely different topics, then you might want to reconsider studying with them. You might choose to study alone instead of studying with that individual or group of people. However, if you have difficulties studying alone, you need to be careful in choosing your study partner.

Example

Tiana has three siblings and lives in a small house. She shares a room with one of her siblings. When she sits down to study, she always gets distracted or interrupted by the sounds of the house. Eventually, she started going to the library to study. After awhile she noticed a group of kids from her school coming to study there as well. She asked to be in their study group. They said yes, and so she started studying with them. After two days of studying with the group, Tiana realized that it wasn't going to work out. They spent the time chatting about class or working quietly on their own things. This didn't work for Tiana, but she liked studying with other people. Tiana found a different study group, and this group worked better for her. They focused on the material they were tasked with learning when they got together and, as a result, they helped each other and did better on class preparation and tests.

11. Procrastination

Learning under pressure becomes difficult when we procrastinate for too long, thereby leaving a shorter period to study material. Procrastination is not recommended when it comes to studying. People sometimes underestimate the time they have to read or accomplish a task. When the time for accomplishing a task is shortened by procrastination, they have difficulty achieving the desired goals. To avoid procrastination schedule your studying or tasks into smaller chunks of time and determine deadlines for accomplishing each of them. Then follow through on your plan. Doing this will help you meet your study targets.

Example

After Tiana and her group worked with each other for a few weeks, a new student asked to join the group. He begged the group to help him with his essay. He had procrastinated until he only had a day to write and turn in his essay. Tiana and the group helped him get the essay done, but Tiana talked to him after study group and offered to help him get more organized, so that he wouldn't have another issue that put him in a bind. He gladly accepted, and, since then, didn't have anymore issues with procrastination. Putting off until tomorrow what you can do today often does not help you achieve what you want to accomplish on the road to success.

CHAPTER SIX

Best Places to Study

Studying in a place with distractions can hamper your ability to focus and get your work done. When you choose a place to study, your ability to learn and focus is greatly increased. It also aids your retentiveness and the speed at which you read. There are many places one can study, but, as we said, concentration is key, and you want to find a place that will help you concentrate when looking for a place to study.

You shouldn't adopt another person's style of study as it relates to study places. What works for them might not work for you, so you should not work hard trying to fit yourself into an environment that may not suit you. If you enjoy a place with soft music playing in the background, then you might want to choose a coffee shop or a bookstore. However, if you'd prefer a quiet location, then the library or a tutoring center may be best. The first three rules about a good study area are: the place should be comfortable, have an appropriate noise level, and should have enough information, whether it is books or electronic resources, access to aid your reading.

1. A library

If you are not comfortable studying in a library, then you just might want to look at other options. However, a library is always quiet, and the librarians accept nothing else. A library is comfortable. The sitting and table arrangements are often good and conducive to studying. Also, diverse books and electronic resources are available, so you will likely find the information you need. Consider also that librarians are there to specifically tend to your studying needs. The library ranks as one of the top key places to study. Consider picking a library closest to you.

2. Your room

Studying in your room is good, and it can easily pass the qualifications of a good study place. The problem and limitations come from having too many neighbors or friends that you can hear or interrupt you with a quick visit or a noisy roommate. Apart from these problems, if they exist, your room is an ideal place for you to study, and you can basically study in comfort. You should ensure you are logged out of social media to improve your concentration.

3. A coffee shop

If you like bliss and comfort, you may like a coffee shop. A coffee shop is the next perfect place for your studying except that it may be noisy. The baristas' music plays early morning and late night and can be very helpful to get you into a reading mood. Also, most coffee shops have Wi-Fi, so you can use your laptop to access information from the Internet.

4. A bookstore

Remember that we mentioned information access as one of the key features of the best study places? Well, information access is usually pretty good at a bookstore. There are thousands of books, magazines, and journals for you to go through to get quick information. Some large bookstores usually have a café as part of their business model, so studying in such a place means that you can help yourself to caffeine or a Panini. Remember, though, to keep this to a minimum as both caffeine and sugar will give you a rush. After awhile it can also lead you a study breakdown. Once the stimulant affects passes, your mental ability tends to drop. Caffeine and sugar is addictive, unhealthy, and will affect you tremendously in the long-term. Bookstores also do not tend to attract crowds unless a special event is happening. They are expected to be relatively quiet in order to serve their customers, so you can read and study without any distractions.

5. An empty classroom

If distractions keep you from reading with your friends. You could consider going to an empty classroom. An empty classroom might not be as comfortable as you would want it to be for reading, but it is a place to get 100% quiet time while studying. Ensure that whatever place you study at, it is one that is secure and safe. Consider a classroom where there are few people and perhaps where a teacher comes in once in a while to check on you.

6. Community center

If a community center is closer to your house than any of the places previously listed, then you should consider it. Most community centers have places (a reserved room) where you can study. Also, the community may have exercising equipment or an exercise room, which is always a plus to help you feel better and improve your concentration after a workout, as long as the workout does not become a distraction.

7. The home of a study partner

If your study partner has a comfortable residence with all the key features of a perfect study place, then it is a viable option. The benefits of studying at your study partner's place are that you get the benefit of studying with someone who shares the same goals as you do and is working just as hard as you are to achieve them. Also, you can share information and lecture notes.

8. The park

Besides studying in your classroom, community center, or even the library, you may want to visit and go to the park to study. Don't forget to take sunscreen, water, and bug spray as well.

9. Tutoring center

Finding a place to study is relatively easy. What you do when you get there is what matters. Do you really study? Do you focus on what you study? If you are constantly having issues focusing, then you might want to use a tutoring center. The only disadvantage is that there may be a fee to enter. Some tutoring centers have tutors or assistants available that can help you learn what you need to learn. Also, there are usually a minimum of distractions at a tutoring center.

10. School lounge

If you are capable of studying with a little noise and ambiance, you might want to consider the school lounge as opposed to the library. Remember, your choice is not a matter of what you prefer, but what will work for you. The lounge may have other students who study there too. Places are designed for specific activities. For example, a basketball court to play ball, the cinema to see movies, the restaurant to eat, and so on. Each place is designed for something specific, so you should try to find places conducive for activities that enhance concentration and the ability to read without too many interruptions. One of those places can be your school's lounge.

CHAPTER SEVEN

Signs That You Have Been Studying Excessively

As students we must study continuously to refresh our memory and keep us abreast of what is happening around us, and, most importantly, to achieve that good grade. Most jobs after graduation will require you to use the study skills you've learned as a student. However, as important as studying is, it should never be at the detriment of your health. This is one key aspect too many students fail to understand.

Learn to balance your study life to include active studying while ensuring that you get enough rest and even recreation or a social life. Taking a break once in a while in-between your study periods will help your brain to settle and absorb the information you are working to understand. It also helps to boost your retentiveness. Sometimes we study so much that we do not know when to stop. We usually see the signs, but do not know what they mean. This chapter is designed to help you recognize the signs of excessive study. When you see these signs, make sure you take a break.

1. You can no longer retain information

When you pick up your book to read, the possibility of you comprehending what is being read is very high because that is the first stage of studying, and your brain is still alert. People differ, and some students can read for 3 to 4 hours without any stress on their retentiveness. What works for you will not necessarily work for another person and vice versa. When you find yourself reading and rereading the same sentence or paragraph over and over, you should take a break.

2. You have had way too much coffee

Coffee is good. In fact, most psychologists recommend drinking caffeine for students who stay up late at night to study and for those who read for long periods of time during the day. However, coffee can be addictive and detrimental to your health. When you find yourself becoming agitated after drinking coffee, you need to step away from that book and the coffee. After awhile you will recognize when you need to take a break.

3. You have tried to solve the same problem over a thousand times and still cannot get it

If you find yourself struggling with the same mathematical problem or some other concept over a long period of time, you probably know how frustrating it can be. Most times the solution to this problem can be found in something explained to you repeatedly, but you just cannot solve it on your own. This is your brain telling you that it's tired and needs a break.

4. Wow! Your eye is twitching

Sometimes twitching occurs with one eye, and it happens when the lower lid of an eye keeps moving up and down on its own. This is very distracting and can make concentrating or retaining information difficult. A twitching eye, or another physical tick, is a sign you have studied for too long, and you need a break. Sometimes a twitching eye arises from staring too long at your digital device. The light from our laptops, phones, and other digital devices can be very dangerous to the eyes if we keep looking at them for too long. This is why we should try as much as possible to limit our reading on these devices and read more on paper. Alternatively, if you are going to be reading with these devices, then you should consider using light glasses to mitigate the detrimental effects on your eyes.

5. Your dreams are about studying

When you start dreaming about studying, then it's appropriate to call that a nightmare. When the majority of what you dream about is studying or engaging in study groups, then you should incorporate other social activities into your schedule to help balance your life.

6. Your family thinks you are missing

Some very diligent students can become so engrossed in studying that they forget they have a family. You should actively, and intentionally, try to balance your life in general. Families matter and so do your friends. Try to schedule your time so you can enjoy these important relationships while, at the same time, succeeding in your effort to study.

7. You no longer know what your friends outside of class look like

If you are always going to the library or to the school lounge to study after class and not socializing with your friends, you need to work at making a well-rounded life. Maintaining friendships outside the classroom is important. You need to take a break from too much studying and try to balance your study life with your social life.

8. You are falling asleep in your class, study groups, or while studying alone

Sleep is a good thing, and it's one of the best ways to rest our brains. When you find yourself sleeping during study times, you have probably deprived yourself of sleep. Falling asleep during study time normally comes with other 'take a break' signs, such as not being able to solve a problem even after having tried several times. Or having a feeling that you are just not retaining what you are reading or trying to remember. When sacrificing sleep in order to achieve a good grade or a well-done report or research, you need to understand the importance of your mental health. Balance your study life. You can.

9. Your significant other is no longer sure of you

Relationships sometimes suffer when you do not take a break from studying. When your significant other begins to complain about your absence in the relationship and starts blaming that on your excessive studying, then you might want to take a break for the sake of your relationship.

10. You feel slow and unable to function after your study sessions

When you strain the brain for too long with a particular activity, the possibility of the brain becoming overloaded can happen. When this occurs the brain cannot accommodate any more learning. You may become slower than usual when engaging in other activities. When you notice that after study sessions you have difficulty fully participating in activities, you should take a long break. Have fun, do something that does not require you to task your brain so much, like watching a movie or just hanging out with friends.

11. Because you cannot take your book into the shower, you fail at other hygienic activities

Your health matters as much as your studies. When you begin to fail to take regular baths, brush your teeth, do your laundry, and/or keep your living space neat and tidy in exchange for excessive studying, then you need to take a break and reorganize your life. If not, you might soon be down, sick and miserable, and won't be able to give as much time to your studying or hygiene as necessary for a balanced life. Taking care of yourself physically and mentally are key to your overall success throughout your college experience.

12. Your new style is pajamas

This is closely related to the previous point. Studying at your house can be good. It is one of the best study places if there are not too many distractions. However, you can have several places to study. You should not feel like you have to only study in one place. If you are not getting up and getting dressed most mornings and choose to lounge around in pajamas, you had better think about finding a new study place.

13. You feel depressed sometimes

Depression can happen when you do not eat regularly or socialize frequently or feel like you have lost control of your life. If you feel a little depressed and realize you are always studying at the same place, you might want to take a break for awhile and visit family or friends. Watch a movie or engage in other fun activities that make you laugh and feel happy.

14. You begin to mix words while reading your notes

This is usually the most obvious of all signs that you need to take a break from studying. Sometimes, mixing up your words might be because you have taken a nap and immediately picked your book up to study it. If you have studied for quite some time, and realize that you have begun mixing words in your head—'what' for 'who,' 'come' for 'corn,' and so on, your brain needs to take a break. It is telling you you need to take a walk or socialize a little bit.

15. Your desk has become full of pizza boxes and monster cans

When you are studying you should always eat to replenish the vitamins and other nutrients. However, having your desk filled with pizza boxes and drinking containers with only a crunched space for you to study tells you just one thing–that you are always stationed at your studying place and have no time for other activities in your life. Learn to balance your life generally. You can have the best grades with a good social life and be a very good and balanced person. It all depends on how you arrange your life and manage your time.

16. Your entire body hurts, especially your back and neck

When you have been sitting for a long time, your back and neck may start to hurt. Try to move around once in a while even while studying. Take a stroll to the end of the corridor and back. Step out and say 'hi' to a neighbor in your building and then go back to your reading. This way you will be stretching muscles and bones likely to hurt when you are in a particular position for too long.

17. Your test scores are not improving

One thing we do not understand when we send information to our brain (study) is that the brain needs some time to process and store information. You can read and understand what you are reading, but then, without your brain storing the information, you you can fail to retain what you have read. When this happens you find yourself back to the same place you began before you started to study. At the end of the day the overall result of this is that you did not do so well studying even though you finished the whole book and did all your assignments. The next time you see any of these signs, take the cue and take a good rest.

Chapter Eight

Effects of Studying Excessively

A lot of people we look to for advice and mentoring often advise us about how much we should study to be successful in life. Parents, siblings, and coaches tell us to study very hard, which is all good. The problem comes when we cannot draw a line on studying obsessively and that affects our mental and physical health. Oftentimes we joke about how studying for long periods keeps us from having a balanced life. But this is all real. We must understand that there is a huge difference between studying well and studying excessively. In the former you are more likely to get your perfect, or at least better, grades while the latter may basically result in less desirable grades. All of us need to understand what excessive studying can do to our mental and physical health.

1. Stress and tension

Cramming too much information into your brain and not taking proper care of yourself can cause your body to give you signs of excessive stress and unwanted tension. Stress is not good for your body or brain, and tensions have made people go blank, especially during tests or making a required presentation. Researchers show that students who study too much become exposed to excessive tension and stress. As a result some people become victims of major heart diseases such as stroke, diabetes, or obesity. Stress can cause high blood pressure, which can lead to a stroke. All of us need to know when to draw the line in our study. We also need to know and realize when we are stressed and tense from too much studying. Apart from all of this, study-induced stress can, in some people, trigger inflammation of the brain, making it impossible for the information to be retained or for the information to be recovered easily. Studying excessively can also cause depression. In fact overworking one's self generally induces diverse heart and body diseases. You should always be conscious of your health while striving to achieve scholastic goals.

2. Higher risks of death

All around the world physical inactivity is the fourth leading cause of death. According to medical research, this particular cause of death is higher among students than other categories of people. When we study we tend to stay stationed at a particular spot, and this strains our body, especially our back and neck. As a result our cardiovascular systems can become compromised at any given time. Sitting for too long can also increase strain on relevant body parts such as the legs, neck, back, and also our eyes. While reading one should move around once in a while to reduce this risk.

3. Underperformance during exams and tests

Underperformance during tests mostly occurs because we have either sacrificed other activities, including our hobbies, if we are focused on just our studies, or we have not studied enough. The effect from sacrificing other activities is that we lose the enthusiasm and zeal to study or learn, which affects our approach to exams and tests. Your hobbies and other activities should not be neglected since this may make you feel unwillingly sluggish when you think about engaging in other activities. Without an overall balanced life, including the things we love to do, there is little or no zeal to do the things we naturally might not want to do, such as study.

4. You begin to overthink

Overthinking is the reality of reading everything and anything. You think of subtle, or small, issues and turn them into big issues. You do not snap out of anxiety or overthinking until you have solved the mystery you've read in a book, even when such issues cannot be solved. This is time-consuming and takes your mind off real issues and people without seeing the need to enable people who do not think the same way as you. You might even sever certain long-term relationships if you are not careful.

5. You have an opinion about virtually everything

Opinions are good. They portray our knowledge of the world, and there are so many controversial issues. We may start to feel that we have an opinion about everything happening in the world. The effect of this is that we become addicted to studying because we cannot let go of not having an idea or opinion about a thing or a person. With time we might be forced into losing ourselves, and the people around us, because we fail to draw a line between knowledge and information. As a result of this, most people can become depressed, and they may, in the long run, lose touch with life and other things and people.

6. You make bad decisions with your money

If you find yourself spending your money on new clothes, entertainment, and recreational activities it can be good, but it can also be detrimental to your wellbeing if it becomes excessive. This is mainly caused by our addictions to things that distract us from being too engrossed with studying, and we forget that other aspects of life are also equally relevant. This can breed poor hygiene habits and a lack of enthusiasm for a properly balanced social life.

7. Procrastination

We can only accomplish so much at a time, and eventually, doing things can become excessive. Studying for very long hours non-stop lengthens the time you spend studying, while diminishing productivity. You spend hours with your books and feel like you get nothing in return. The overall affect of this is that you give less time to things that should normally take the space your extra study time is taking. You may start to feel tired and notice your brain cannot receive or store any more information, but you remain too determined to ensure you finish up that book or that chapter. You consume the time you should have spent doing some other activity. Doing this continuously can lead to being addicted to, and comfortable with, procrastinations.

8. Malnutrition

You get out of bed in the morning and decide to take a shower, which you rush through because you cannot wait to start studying, even though you spent the previous night reading and going through your notes. You gulp down a cup of coffee and head off for the library. Then you sit consuming volumes and volumes of pages, and before it's time for lunch, your stomach is churning, but you ignore it. You are basically not eating any food before studying, which is not good for your health.

Malnutrition does not only appear with eating wrongly; it also comes from not eating at all. Serious complications can come about if you eat junk food and drink soda to hold yourself until dinner-time. This habit will reflect on your nutrition, your retentiveness, and your general ability to absorb information. Sacrificing healthy nutrition while you study is never a good decision as it drains the brain and leaves you weaker when you try to recollect what you have studied. Eat well, and, in fact, you should eat more during study time than at any other time. Do not forget to consume enough fruits too and avoid junk food as much as possible.

9. Memory loss

A lot of medications and over the counter drugs can cause memory loss, including anti-depressants and anti-anxiety prescriptions, or even alcohol. Some people take flu drugs to keep active when they should probably be resting. The counter-productive effect of this is that the brain is conditioned to make it through dire situations – which is more like traveling a long way on a very bad tire. The brain becomes overworked. When too many drugs are taken, memory loss can occur.

This chapter is not trying to downplay the importance of studying. In fact, studying is really, really important. You should adopt good study habits and be able to keep a balance with other activities in your life. Using these tips you will be able to absorb information and retain it, building up the knowledge you have inside yourself. Someone who has learned how to study also becomes increasingly better at the process of learning. Furthermore, the tips in this book will help you to recall the information stored when it is needed.

Other major effects of excessive study include addiction to drugs and/or coffee, mental diseases such as amnesia.

Chapter Nine

Keeping Up With Online Learning During The COVID-19 Pandemic

One of the most important aspects of studying currently is the growth of online education. How do you succeed when you either want to study at home or are forced to do so?

Ripple effects of the coronavirus pandemic can be seen in the worldwide educational sector as students all over the world have been forced out of school. Because of the crisis, educational leaders are trying to manage the situation and find new approaches to continuously provide quality education to students and cushion the pandemic's effects on education.

This has meant that most schools have taken up distance learning or online classes for their students. Classes are now being held on several apps like Zoom or FaceTime and other similar apps, with teachers doing their best to provide resources for their students. Despite being a great idea, there are still several challenges with the online learning plan, especially when students need to master studying using new, unfamiliar learning tools.

While many large lecturers are able to make a smooth transition online, some can't because they are supposed to be lab courses with an experimental component and hands-on. Schools continue to seek effective ways to ensure that online classes provide student success.

What seems evident is that the new development is taking its toll on students as many do not know how to adjust to the new method of learning.

Students who find themselves trying to learn online in the COVID-19 pandemic have been forced to develop a new set of concentration and study skills to maintain their place in the classroom. Sadly, not all students are able to participate for several reasons. Although adjusting to the new reality is not a walk in the park, making changes will take quite some time and effort. There are tips, however, that can help students whose learning has moved online.

1. Remain Disciplined

Obviously your home does not have the features of your school, but you are still a student. That means you have to finish your course load in the same amount of time you used to complete it prior to the pandemic. But being at home, there is a high chance of distraction and interruption; therefore, a focused mind will lead to distance learning success.

To maintain concentration, create a workspace or study space for yourself and develop a study schedule. You can convert the home dining table to a desk, and before class begins, prep yourself with some last-minute stretching maneuvers to give you the "preparing for class" feeling. This helps your mind to settle in and prepare to study.

Not only that, using calendar apps to schedule the time for your classes and visualizing what you've developed for the week can be useful too, especially if using the calendar spp becomes a habit. Small manageable time frames help maintain focus.

Participating actively in live online lectures and study groups so that you are included in the routine aspects of online learning is essential. Unfortunately, learning online eliminates social cues that may come with having your classes in the traditional sense. When participating in class, it is usually better to prepare your thoughts, then write them down before posting them, to ensure clear communication. Also, keep your phone out of your reach until you are done with classes.

2. Maintain Flexibility

When your classes have taken different forms, including videos, online lectures or reading series, you also have to study using a digital library. The adjustment from classroom to online learning is smooth if you are flexible and accommodate these changes.

There are times when you need to adjust without advance notice. For example, you may be working online and lose internet connection, leaving you unable to proceed. A better practice would be to download course materials so they are accessible offline at a later time. Ensure you have your instructors' contact information, phone numbers, and email addresses handy as you may have to contact them about any technical difficulties and challenges that you may face.

Also, look up additional learning resources online as well as the ones you're provided. Take the time to do as much research on the subject matter discussed in class, and develop a filing system of recently researched information to have it readily accessible.

3. Time Management is Crucial

Assess your situation in each of your classes and set a reminder of exams and deadlines. Dealing with the scheduled times for exams, classes, online discussions, zoom sessions, or other requirements is essential if you are going to succeed at online learning. Since you do not have reminders delivered during classtimes with online learning, you have to work on creating your own reminders.

When you are consistent with logging into your online classes every day, you have the opportunity to keep up with assignments, quizzes, and even exams even if the deadlines and dates for some of them change as you work through the class material. You do need to be aware that online teachers do change deadlines and dates sometimes, and you have to be alert enough to pick up on those changes.

Once you're updated, organize yourself and design a plan to finish your work and prepare a schedule to help you navigate between being present for virtual classes and doing assignments and projects.

4. Don't Pressure Others

No matter how seamless you expect the online learning process to be, it will be successful if you exercise patience. Most of your instructors are trying to understand the online learning process as much as you are, especially if they became online teachers as a result of the coronavirus emergency. Most of them were-given only days or a week to transition to distance learning. This is really different compared to the longer time they are accustomed to having in order to prepare for classes. Some instructors, of course, teach online because they prefer to teach that way, and you can expect those teachers to be more proficient at using online teaching tools.

If your instructors are new to online teaching and learning as you are, you have to adjust if you have problems with the courses and accessing study materials as your instructors are also trying their best to make it work. Don't be hard on yourself if you feel you're struggling to learn. Most people are unable to concentrate well because they're thinking about other serious challenges during the pandemic, so try new ways of maintaining concentration. Enlist the help of those around you like, family and close friends, and let them know how to help you achieve your study goals.

5. Take Things in Stride

It is important that you maintain a good level of seriousness, but go easy. Do not spend the entire day staring at your computer screen since that is bad for your brain and body. Plan hourly breaks in your schedule and spend the time being active. You can make coffee, stretch, or do any other activity to take your mind off studying during breaks.

If you are taking a course that requires you to use simulations instead of performing the actual hands-on activity, try your best to imitate the real activity as much as you can. Even though you may be doing more theory based assignments, instead of actual hands-on activities still make it count.

6. Stay Connected

Prior to the pandemic, you were on campus where you could walk around, make enquiries, participate in study groups, mingle with friends, and visit tutors. Such activities that were part of the learning process can still be maintained in online learning.

To make distance learning work, it's best to stay in contact with your instructors in order to ask questions and submit complaints (if any), be active in online discussions that take place in your course, participate in virtual study sessions and maintain contact with your colleagues and classmates through social media, phone calls, email, or texts.

CONCLUSION

The way we study and how well we strategize for our study is important. Taking notes is not enough. Without adequate study skills to effectively internalize information, we are left in the same position prior to our studying. This is the major cause of reading for long hours non-stop, not understanding what you've read, and not making a good grade. Apart from capturing facts from your texts and trying to put them down in your own words, you also need to master reading strategies and skills, including time management. This is all part of the strategic study plan. Capturing of information comes only when you have gathered the underlying information in your text before even taking notes. Best results can be achieved without sacrificing endless hours and being buried in excessive studying. Remember, the importance of working towards a well-balanced life is part of the secret to achieving key study skills while taking your studies very seriously. Plan and strategize as you work to getting the best grade, just as you would for every other effort you are enthusiastic about.

The expectation is that this book will help you learn study skills needed to achieve your academic goals. Hopefully, you are now armed with the necessary skills you need. Studying effectively is not going to be easy, and you will need to stick to any plan you make. Good Luck!

ABOUT THE AUTHOR

Christine Reidhead

Christine Reidhead is an avid seeker of knowledge and a zealous humanitarian who shares an incredible passion for the art of serving the community.

Serving as an advocate of education, she aims to enlighten the lives of underserved communities. Christine wants to ignite a positive change among the masses through her passion for community service and the love of sharing others' life stories.

She is a proud mother to two wonderful boys and strives to be an inspiration to all.

Christine presently serves as a Business Professor, Department Chair of Business, Faculty Vice President and Project Manager funded by a United States Department of Transportation Grant.

She is the Founder and CEO of <u>AfrikRising Nonprofit Organization</u>. Christine is the author of *Get That Job! ACE Your JOB Interview — Every Time! and How to Improve Study Habits!*

Want to ace your next job interview? Do you need an edge over the competition? This quick, easy guide will help you throughout the job interview process.

Purchase it on Amazon.

STUDENT

LESSON

PLANNER

THIS PLANNER BELONGS TO

_____

_____

_____

PERSONAL DETAILS

NAME	
ADDRESS	
EMAIL	
PHONE NO.	

OTHER DETAILS

CLASS SCHEDULE

TIME	SUBJECT

MONTH AT A GLANCE

SUBJECT	MONDAY	TUESDAY	WEDNESDAY	THURSDAY	FRIDAY

HOMEWORK PLANNER

SUBJECT	MONDAY	TUESDAY	WEDNESDAY	THURSDAY	FRIDAY

WEEKLY LESSON TOPICS

SUBJECT	MONDAY	TUESDAY	WEDNESDAY	THURSDAY	FRIDAY

WEEKLY CLASS ASSIGNMENT

SUBJECT	MONDAY	TUESDAY	WEDNESDAY	THURSDAY	FRIDAY

WEEKLY CLASS ASSIGNMENT

SUBJECT	MONDAY	TUESDAY	WEDNESDAY	THURSDAY	FRIDAY

CLASS #1

TOPICS FOR THE WEEK

MONDAY	Notes
TUESDAY	
WEDNESDAY	
THURSDAY	
FRIDAY	

CLASS #2

TOPICS FOR THE WEEK

MONDAY	*Notes*
TUESDAY	
WEDNESDAY	
THURSDAY	
FRIDAY	

CLASS #3

TOPICS FOR THE WEEK

MONDAY	Notes
TUESDAY	
WEDNESDAY	
THURSDAY	
FRIDAY	

CLASS #4

TOPICS FOR THE WEEK

MONDAY	Notes
TUESDAY	
WEDNESDAY	
THURSDAY	
FRIDAY	

CLASS #5

TOPICS FOR THE WEEK

MONDAY	Notes
TUESDAY	
WEDNESDAY	
THURSDAY	
FRIDAY	

CLASS #6

TOPICS FOR THE WEEK

MONDAY	Notes
TUESDAY	
WEDNESDAY	
THURSDAY	
FRIDAY	

CLASS #7

TOPICS FOR THE WEEK

MONDAY	Notes
TUESDAY	
WEDNESDAY	
THURSDAY	
FRIDAY	

CLASS #8

TOPICS FOR THE WEEK

MONDAY	Notes
TUESDAY	
WEDNESDAY	
THURSDAY	
FRIDAY	

CLASS #9

TOPICS FOR THE WEEK

MONDAY	Notes
TUESDAY	
WEDNESDAY	
THURSDAY	
FRIDAY	

CLASS #10

TOPICS FOR THE WEEK

MONDAY	Notes
TUESDAY	
WEDNESDAY	
THURSDAY	
FRIDAY	

CLASS #11

TOPICS FOR THE WEEK

MONDAY	Notes
TUESDAY	
WEDNESDAY	
THURSDAY	
FRIDAY	

JANUARY

SUNDAY	MONDAY	TUESDAY	WEDNESDAY

THURSDAY	FRIDAY	SATURDAY	TODO

SUBJECT:

MONDAY	
TUESDAY	
WEDNESDAY	
THURSDAY	
FRIDAY	

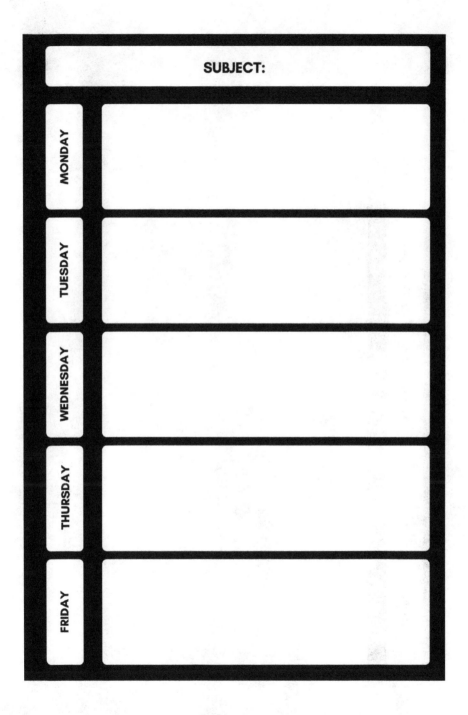

SUBJECT:

MONDAY

TUESDAY

WEDNESDAY

THURSDAY

FRIDAY

SUBJECT:

MONDAY	
TUESDAY	
WEDNESDAY	
THURSDAY	
FRIDAY	

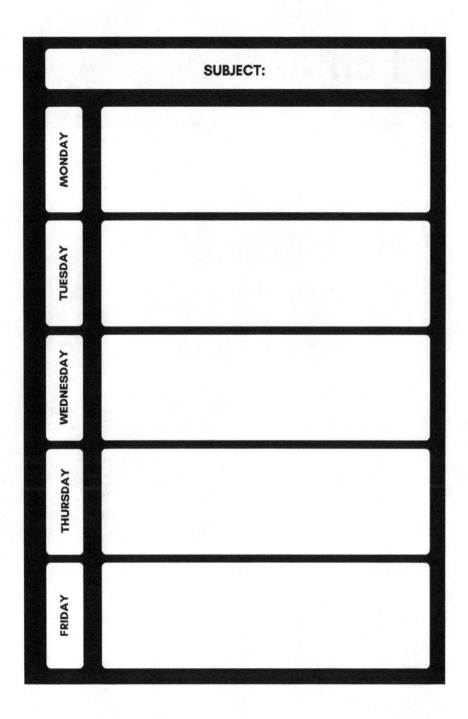

SUBJECT:

MONDAY

TUESDAY

WEDNESDAY

THURSDAY

FRIDAY

FEBRUARY

SUNDAY	MONDAY	TUESDAY	WEDNESDAY

THURSDAY	FRIDAY	SATURDAY	TODO

SUBJECT:

MONDAY	
TUESDAY	
WEDNESDAY	
THURSDAY	
FRIDAY	

116

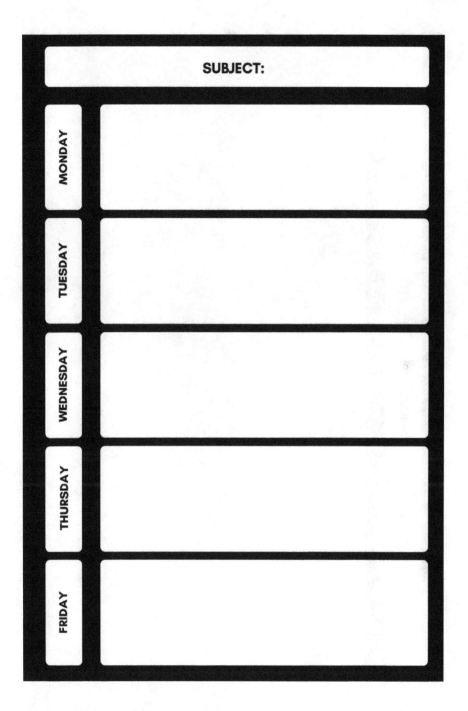

SUBJECT:

MONDAY

TUESDAY

WEDNESDAY

THURSDAY

FRIDAY

118

	SUBJECT:
MONDAY	
TUESDAY	
WEDNESDAY	
THURSDAY	
FRIDAY	

MARCH

SUNDAY	MONDAY	TUESDAY	WEDNESDAY

THURSDAY	FRIDAY	SATURDAY	TODO

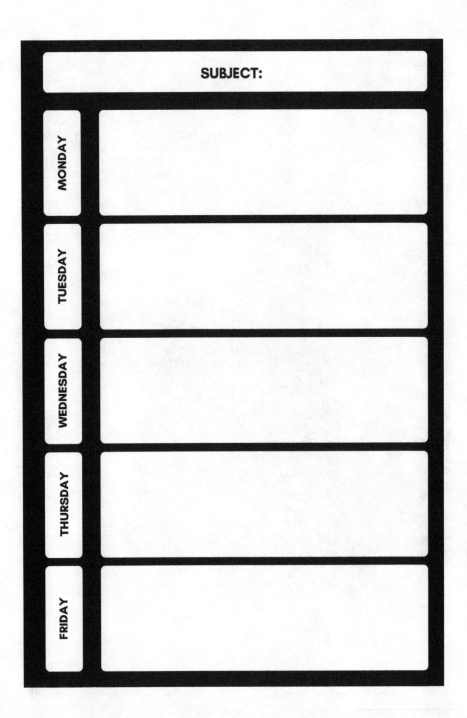

SUBJECT:

MONDAY

TUESDAY

WEDNESDAY

THURSDAY

FRIDAY

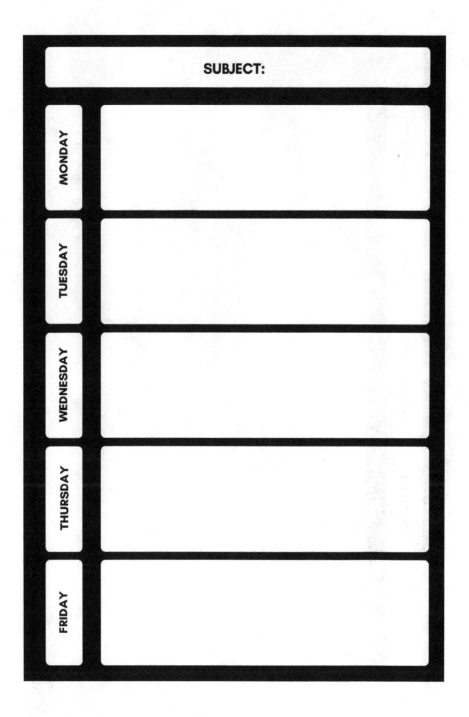

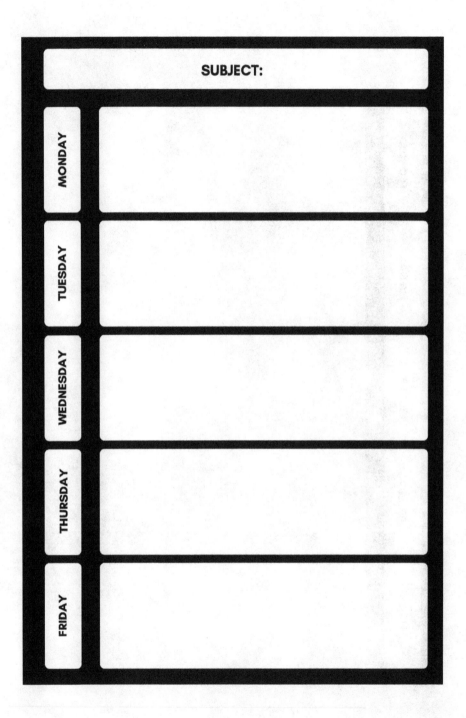

SUBJECT:

MONDAY

TUESDAY

WEDNESDAY

THURSDAY

FRIDAY

SUBJECT:

MONDAY	
TUESDAY	
WEDNESDAY	
THURSDAY	
FRIDAY	

APRIL

SUNDAY	MONDAY	TUESDAY	WEDNESDAY

THURSDAY	FRIDAY	SATURDAY	TODO

SUBJECT:

MONDAY

TUESDAY

WEDNESDAY

THURSDAY

FRIDAY

SUBJECT:

MONDAY	
TUESDAY	
WEDNESDAY	
THURSDAY	
FRIDAY	

	SUBJECT:
MONDAY	
TUESDAY	
WEDNESDAY	
THURSDAY	
FRIDAY	

SUBJECT:

MONDAY	
TUESDAY	
WEDNESDAY	
THURSDAY	
FRIDAY	

MAY

SUNDAY	MONDAY	TUESDAY	WEDNESDAY

THURSDAY	FRIDAY	SATURDAY	TODO

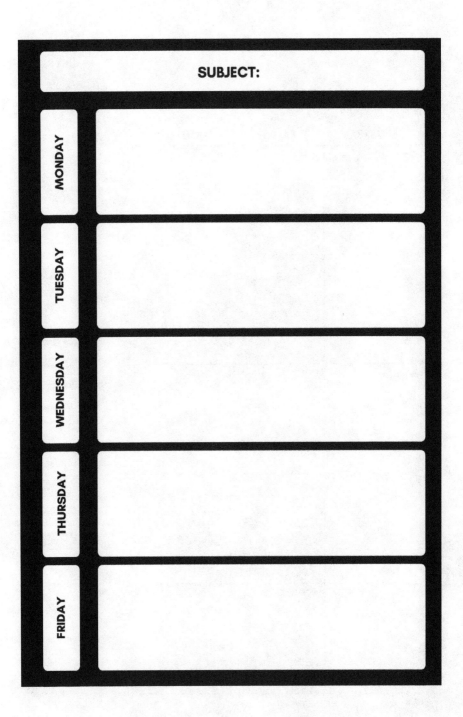

SUBJECT:

MONDAY

TUESDAY

WEDNESDAY

THURSDAY

FRIDAY

SUBJECT:

MONDAY	
TUESDAY	
WEDNESDAY	
THURSDAY	
FRIDAY	

SUBJECT:

MONDAY	
TUESDAY	
WEDNESDAY	
THURSDAY	
FRIDAY	

SUBJECT:

MONDAY	
TUESDAY	
WEDNESDAY	
THURSDAY	
FRIDAY	

137

JUNE

SUNDAY	MONDAY	TUESDAY	WEDNESDAY

THURSDAY	FRIDAY	SATURDAY	TODO

SUBJECT:

MONDAY

TUESDAY

WEDNESDAY

THURSDAY

FRIDAY

SUBJECT:

MONDAY	
TUESDAY	
WEDNESDAY	
THURSDAY	
FRIDAY	

SUBJECT:

MONDAY	
TUESDAY	
WEDNESDAY	
THURSDAY	
FRIDAY	

SUBJECT:

MONDAY	
TUESDAY	
WEDNESDAY	
THURSDAY	
FRIDAY	

JULY

SUNDAY	MONDAY	TUESDAY	WEDNESDAY

THURSDAY	FRIDAY	SATURDAY	TODO

SUBJECT:

MONDAY	
TUESDAY	
WEDNESDAY	
THURSDAY	
FRIDAY	

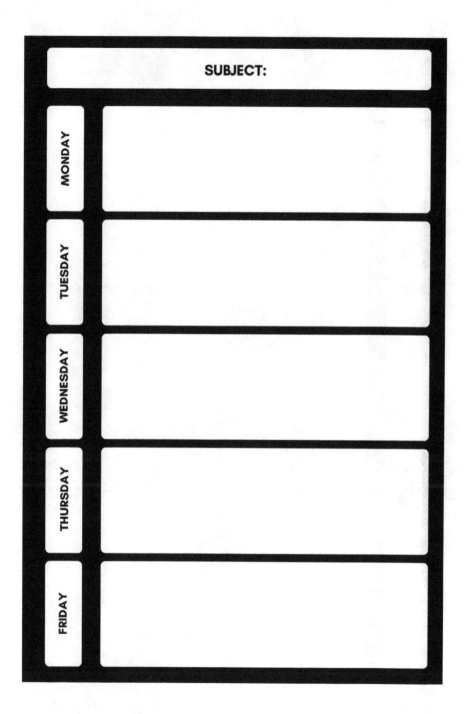

147

SUBJECT:

MONDAY	
TUESDAY	
WEDNESDAY	
THURSDAY	
FRIDAY	

SUBJECT:

MONDAY

TUESDAY

WEDNESDAY

THURSDAY

FRIDAY

AUGUST

SUNDAY	MONDAY	TUESDAY	WEDNESDAY

THURSDAY	FRIDAY	SATURDAY	TODO

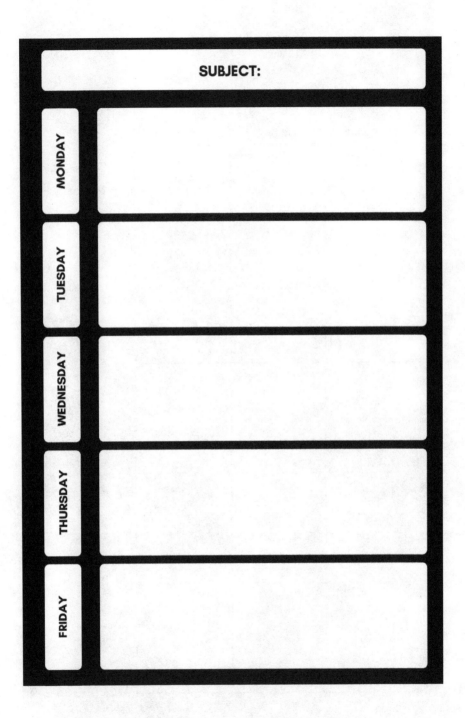

SUBJECT:

MONDAY

TUESDAY

WEDNESDAY

THURSDAY

FRIDAY

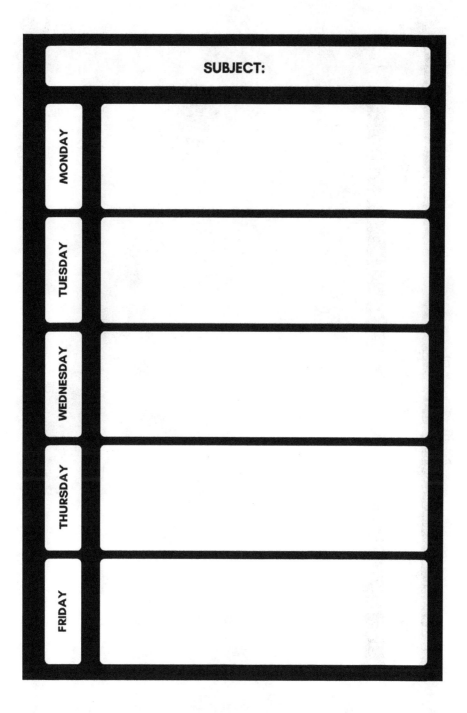

SUBJECT:

MONDAY

TUESDAY

WEDNESDAY

THURSDAY

FRIDAY

SUBJECT:

MONDAY	
TUESDAY	
WEDNESDAY	
THURSDAY	
FRIDAY	

SUBJECT:

MONDAY	
TUESDAY	
WEDNESDAY	
THURSDAY	
FRIDAY	

SEPTEMBER

SUNDAY	MONDAY	TUESDAY	WEDNESDAY

THURSDAY	FRIDAY	SATURDAY	TODO

SUBJECT:

MONDAY	
TUESDAY	
WEDNESDAY	
THURSDAY	
FRIDAY	

SUBJECT:

MONDAY

TUESDAY

WEDNESDAY

THURSDAY

FRIDAY

SUBJECT:

MONDAY

TUESDAY

WEDNESDAY

THURSDAY

FRIDAY

SUBJECT:

MONDAY

TUESDAY

WEDNESDAY

THURSDAY

FRIDAY

161

OCTOBER

SUNDAY	MONDAY	TUESDAY	WEDNESDAY

THURSDAY	FRIDAY	SATURDAY	TODO

SUBJECT:

MONDAY	
TUESDAY	
WEDNESDAY	
THURSDAY	
FRIDAY	

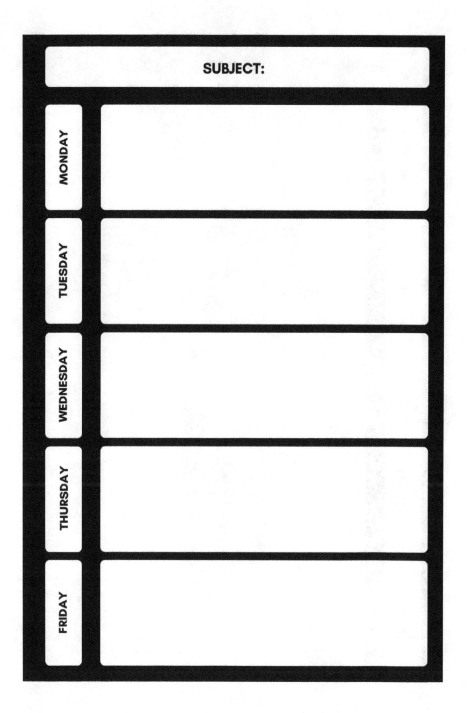

SUBJECT:

MONDAY

TUESDAY

WEDNESDAY

THURSDAY

FRIDAY

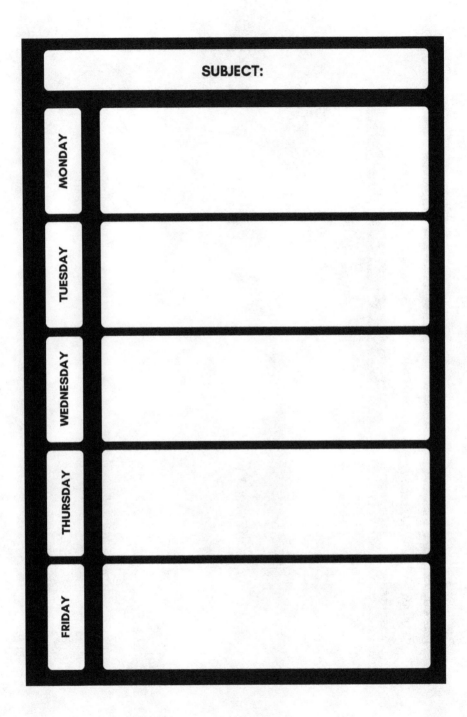

SUBJECT:

MONDAY	
TUESDAY	
WEDNESDAY	
THURSDAY	
FRIDAY	

167

NOVEMBER

SUNDAY	MONDAY	TUESDAY	WEDNESDAY

THURSDAY	FRIDAY	SATURDAY	TODO

SUBJECT:

MONDAY	
TUESDAY	
WEDNESDAY	
THURSDAY	
FRIDAY	

SUBJECT:

MONDAY	
TUESDAY	
WEDNESDAY	
THURSDAY	
FRIDAY	

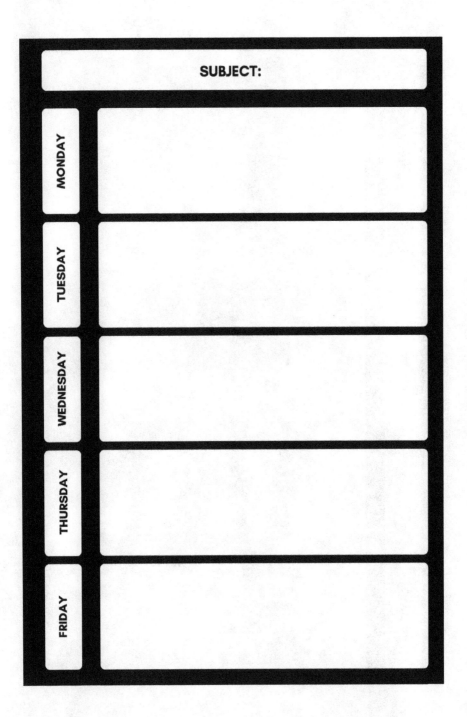

SUBJECT:

MONDAY

TUESDAY

WEDNESDAY

THURSDAY

FRIDAY

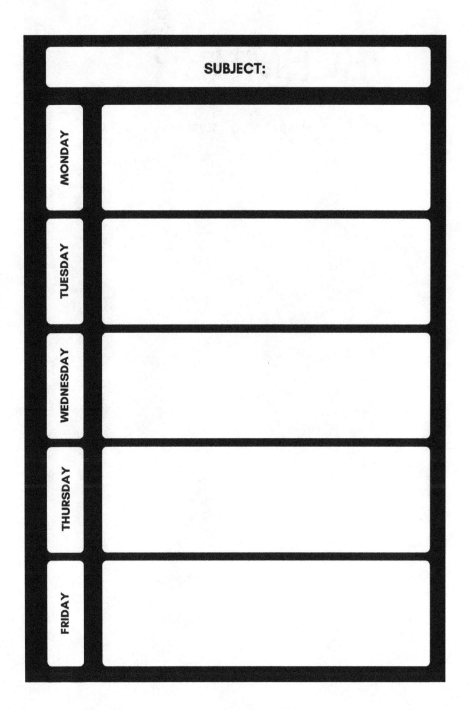

DECEMBER

SUNDAY	MONDAY	TUESDAY	WEDNESDAY

THURSDAY	FRIDAY	SATURDAY	TODO

SUBJECT:

MONDAY

TUESDAY

WEDNESDAY

THURSDAY

FRIDAY

SUBJECT:

MONDAY

TUESDAY

WEDNESDAY

THURSDAY

FRIDAY

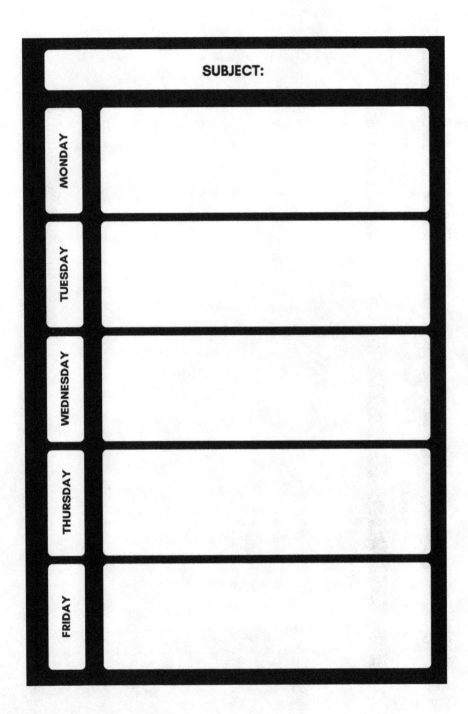

SUBJECT:

MONDAY

TUESDAY

WEDNESDAY

THURSDAY

FRIDAY

SUBJECT:

MONDAY	
TUESDAY	
WEDNESDAY	
THURSDAY	
FRIDAY	

NOTES

NOTES

NOTES

NOTES

Course Overview

SUBJECT:	
TIME:	
LOCATION:	
TEACHER:	
OFFICE HOURS:	
CONTACT INFO:	

SUBJECT:	
TIME:	
LOCATION:	
TEACHER:	
OFFICE HOURS:	
CONTACT INFO:	

SUBJECT:	
TIME:	
LOCATION:	
TEACHER:	
OFFICE HOURS:	
CONTACT INFO:	

SUBJECT:	
TIME:	
LOCATION:	
TEACHER:	
OFFICE HOURS:	
CONTACT INFO:	

Course Goals

COURSE: _____

WEEK	
1	
2	
3	
4	
5	
6	
7	
8	
9	
10	
11	
12	
13	
14	

COORDINATOR

CONTACT INFORMATION

CREDIT POINTS

REQUIRED ATTENDANCE

DUE DATES

EXAM DATES

Semester Overview

SEMESTER: _____   DATE: _____

WEEK			
1			
2			
3			
4			
5			
6			
7			
8			
9			
10			
11			
12			
13			
14			

Weekly Timetable

	MONDAY	TUESDAY	WEDNESDAY	THURSDAY	FRIDAY
8 AM					
9 AM					
10 AM					
11 AM					
12 PM					
1 PM					
2 PM					
3 PM					
4 PM					
5 PM					
6 PM					
7 PM					
8 PM					
9 PM					
10 PM					

Semester Dashboard

SEMESTER SUBJECTS	IMPORTANT INFORMATION

SEMESTER GOALS	COLOR COMBINATION

SEMESTER ACHIEVEMENTS	TEACHER CONTACT INFORMATION

Study Guide Per Subject

Semester Goals

SEMESTER:

SEMESTER GOAL	PROGRESS TRACKER			
1	25 %	50 %	75 %	100 %
2	25 %	50 %	75 %	100 %
3	25 %	50 %	75 %	100 %
4	25 %	50 %	75 %	100 %
5	25 %	50 %	75 %	100 %

GOAL 1	GOAL 2	GOAL 3	GOAL 4	GOAL 5

NOTES	GOAL REFLECTION	YES/NO
	I set achievable goals	
	I planned out how I could achieve those goals	
	I tracked my progress each week	
	I could do better at achieving goals next semester	

Time Management Method Tracker

DATE: _____

TOP 3 PRIORITIES	TARGET SESSION	COMPLETED SESSION	TIME SPENT
1			
2			
3			

TIME STARTED	TIME FINISHED	TASK

BREAKS	NOTES

Exam Checklist

EXAM PERIOD:

SUBJECT	DATE / TIME	PERCENTAGE OF FINAL GRADE	DONE

SUBJECT	SUPPLIES TO BRING

Group Project Planner

SUBJECT:

DATE ISSUED: DUE DATE:

STUDENT NAME	ROLE	CONTACT INFO

NAME	TASK	DEADLINE	STRUCTURE

NOTES	QUESTIONS

Supplier Organizer

SUPPLY NAME	STORE/BRAND	QUANTITY	PRICE	BOUGHT

Project Planner

DATE:

TASK DESCRIPTION	KEY INFO

DATE	PROJECT TO DO LIST

NOTES	PROGRESS	
	25 %	50 %
	75 %	100 %
	Completed	
	Submitted	

Reading Journal

TITLE:	
AUTHOR:	
DATE STARTED:	DATE FINISHED:

COMMENTS AND THOUGHTS

TITLE:	
AUTHOR:	
DATE STARTED:	DATE FINISHED:

COMMENTS AND THOUGHTS

Books to Read

TOPIC	BOOK TITLE

Important Quotes

PERSON	QUOTE	PAGE #

Reading Summary

SUBJECT:

READING NAME	AUTHOR	CITATION

ARGUMENT/CONCEPT	EVIDENCE	EXPLANATION

MORE READINGS TO RESEARCH

Reading Summary

WEEK NO.

READING/ARTICLE NAME	SUMMARY

Chapter Summary

SUBJECT:

CHAPTER NUMBER	PAGE NUMBER	✓	TEXTBOOK CHECKLIST
			Read through chapter
			Highlighted
			Taken notes

KEY POINTS	SUMMARY

KEY WORDS	IMPORTANT QUESTIONS

Grade Overview

SUBJECT:	
GOAL GRADE:	FINAL GRADE:

TASK TITLE	GOAL GRADE	ACTUAL GRADE	COMMENTS

NOTES:

Assessment Tracker

TASK TITLE	DUE DATE	COMPLETE	GRADE

Assessment Breakdown

SUBJECT:

ASSESSMENT DESCRIPTION	ADDITIONAL INFORMATION

DATE	TASK DESCRIPTION

NOTES	PROGRESS	
	25 %	50 %
	75 %	100 %
	Completed	
	Submitted	

Assessment Task Reflection

SUBJECT: _____ GOAL GRADE: _____

TASK NAME: _____ ACTUAL GRADE: _____

REFLECTION	1 = AGREE/ 5 = DISAGREE				
I started at an appropriate time	1	2	3	4	5
I took time to plan and prepare my workings	1	2	3	4	5
I reviewed the marking criteria/guidelines	1	2	3	4	5
I was organized for the task	1	2	3	4	5
I understood the task and what was expected	1	2	3	4	5
This was my best work	1	2	3	4	5
My effort is reflected in the grade I received	1	2	3	4	5
Overall, I am happy with this assessment	1	2	3	4	5

This task took me (hours, days, and weeks):

It was or wasn't enough time:

What I have learned most from this assessment task:

What I found most challenging about this task:

My strengths and weakness in this task were:

Next time I will:

My methods to improve are:

Revision Checklist

TOPIC	AFTER CLASS	AFTER 24HRS	ONE WEEK	ONE MONTH

Study Session Reflection

STUDY SESSION	METHODS	TIME	EFFECTIVENESS
			/ 10
			/ 10
			/ 10
			/ 10
			/ 10
			/ 10
			/ 10
			/ 10
			/ 10
			/ 10
			/ 10
			/ 10
			/ 10
			/ 10
			/ 10

Study Method Guide & Checklist

SUBJECT: _____

STRATEGY	DONE
1. Create a color code for writing and/or highlighting	
2. Organized study materials	
3. Set up a study space	
4. Review typed or written notes	
5. Create a mind-map	
6. Highlight materials (keywords only)	
7. Use flashcards for: vocabulary, question and answer, summaries	
8. Create a study guide	
9. Answer practice questions	
10. Recite information aloud	
11. Summarize topics on to a flashcard or post-it note	
12. Participate in a group study session	
13. Review past homework or worksheets	
14. Do past papers	
15. Make a timeline	
16. Create mnemonic devices for memorizing	
17. Add in diagrams to your notes	
18. Search additional resources (e.g. Youtube, Khan Academy, BBC Bitesize, Crash course)	
19. Record yourself speaking and reciting information	
20. Read sample answers	
21. Apply concepts and theories to real life situations	
22. Time-lapse your study session	
23. Write practice essays	
24. Compare notes with friends	
25. Do a timed response to questions	
26. Read your textbook, flashcards or summary notes before bed	
27. Use the time management method	

Essay Planner

SUBJECT:

QUESTIONS	KEY INFO

INTRODUCTION

BODY ONE	BODY TWO	BODY THREE

NOTES

Essay Planner

SUBJECT:

QUESTIONS	THESIS STATEMENT

POINT ONE:

POINT TWO:

POINT THREE:

POINT FOUR:

NOTES

Essay Checklist

PART 1: UNDERSTANDING THE BRIEF

○ I have read through the essay brief and understand what I have to do

○ I have read and understand the grading guidelines and how I can achieve top grades

○ I have written down the due date and have set reminders

○ I know the requirements, such as word or page limit, required references

○ I have annotated the brief with some of my first ideas and thoughts

PART 2: CREATING A DRAFT

○ I have come up with a thesis in response to the essay question

○ I have created an outline using the essay planner

○ I have began to research talking points, sources, evidence, etc

○ I have outlined a structure to my essay - for example picking the number of paragraphs

PART 3: WRITING UP THE ESSAY

○ I have finished a draft with each of my points documented and planned

○ I have written an introduction

○ I have written body paragraphs (amount is optional)

○ I have written a conclusion

○ I have included required materials - for example: statistics, examples, case studies, sources, opinions, etc

PART 4: PROOFREADING THE ESSAY

○ I have proofread the essay (more than once)

○ I have checked the word or limit to ensure I'm within the range

○ I have used Grammarly.com or Google Translate to pick up minor errors I may have missed

○ I have had a friend or family member read my essay

PART 5: FINAL TOUCHES

○ I have referenced correctly all the way through

○ I have written an introduction

○ I have documented all my references/sources in a bibliography or reference list

○ I have used the required amount of references

○ I have not plagiarized content from another source

PART 6: SUBMISSION

○ I know where and when to submit the essay - either electronically or as a printed copied

○ I have submitted the final draft

Reference Planner

NO. OF REQUIRED REFERENCES	NO. OF FINAL REFERENCES	REFERENCING FORMAT

CITATION INFORMATION (AUTHOR, TITLE, DATE, PUBLISHED, ETC)	CITED

Definitions

SUBJECT:

WORD	DEFINITION

Formulas

SUBJECT:

FORMULA	MEANING / USES

Equations

SUBJECT:

EQUATIONS	MEANING / USES

Language Vocabulary

VOCABULARY	TRANSLATION

Timeline of Events

SUBJECT:

DATE	EVENT

Questions

SUBJECT:

TOPIC	WHAT I DON'T UNDERSTAND	WHAT I'VE TRIED

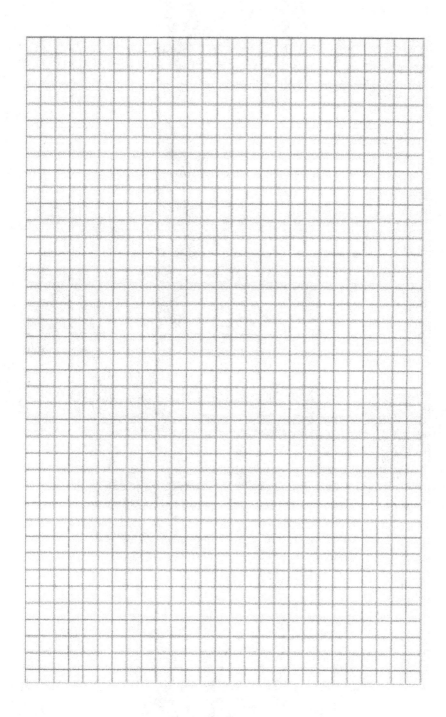

NOTES

Study Strategy DESIGNER

	STEPS	PROGRESS TRACKER		✓
1				
2				
3				
4				
5				
6				
7				
8				
9				
10				
11				
12				
13				
14				
15				
16				
17				
18				
19				
20				
21				

Study CHART

COURSE: _____

	SUBJECT / TOPIC	TIME STUDIED	20%	40%	60%	80%	100%	✓
1								○
2								○
3								○
4								○
5								○
6								○
7								○
8								○
9								○
10								○
11								○
12								○
13								○
14								○
15								○
16								○
17								○
18								○
19								○
20								○

Study PLANNER

EXAM/TIME:

Subjects to Study	Exam/Test Date	Efficiency
		Grade of the day
1		
2		
3		

TOPICS / CHAPTERS   PROGRESS TRACKER

Hourly Study PLANNER

SEMESTER: EXAM/TIME:

	00 – 15	15 – 30	30 – 45	45 – 00
5 AM				
6 AM				
7 AM				
8 AM				
9 AM				
10 AM				
11 AM				
12 PM				
1 PM				
2 PM				
3 PM				
4 PM				
5 PM				
6 PM				
7 PM				
8 PM				
9 PM				
10 PM				
11 PM				
12 AM				

Subjects to Study

1

2

3

Color Codes

Topics / Chapters

Study GUIDE

QUESTION	ANSWER

Semester CHECKLIST

SEMESTER: _____

COURSE ✓

_____ ▢
_____ ▢
_____ ▢
_____ ▢
_____ ▢

COURSE ✓

_____ ▢
_____ ▢
_____ ▢
_____ ▢
_____ ▢

COURSE ✓

_____ ▢
_____ ▢
_____ ▢
_____ ▢
_____ ▢

COURSE ✓

_____ ▢
_____ ▢
_____ ▢
_____ ▢
_____ ▢

COURSE ✓

_____ ▢
_____ ▢
_____ ▢
_____ ▢
_____ ▢

COURSE ✓

_____ ▢
_____ ▢
_____ ▢
_____ ▢
_____ ▢

Semester PLANNER

SEMESTER:

START DATE: END DATE:

CLASS/COURSE	TEACHER	LOCATION	CREDIT

TIMETABLE

	MONDAY	TUESDAY	WEDNESDAY	THURSDAY	FRIDAY
-					
-					
-					
-					
-					
-					
-					
-					
-					
-					

Course KEYPOINTS

COURSE:

TOPIC	SUMMARY

Exam CHECKLIST

SEMESTER: _____

COURSE	TIME AND DATE	CLASSROOM	SUPPLIES	DONE	FINAL GRADE

Semester IMPORTANT DATES

JANUARY
- ☐
- ☐
- ☐
- ☐
- ☐
- ☐
- ☐

FEBRUARY
- ☐
- ☐
- ☐
- ☐
- ☐
- ☐
- ☐

MARCH
- ☐
- ☐
- ☐
- ☐
- ☐
- ☐
- ☐

APRIL
- ☐
- ☐
- ☐
- ☐
- ☐
- ☐
- ☐

MAY
- ☐
- ☐
- ☐
- ☐
- ☐
- ☐
- ☐

JUNE
- ☐
- ☐
- ☐
- ☐
- ☐
- ☐
- ☐

JULY
- ☐
- ☐
- ☐
- ☐
- ☐
- ☐
- ☐

AUGUST
- ☐
- ☐
- ☐
- ☐
- ☐
- ☐
- ☐

SEPTEMBER
- ☐
- ☐
- ☐
- ☐
- ☐
- ☐
- ☐

OCTOBER
- ☐
- ☐
- ☐
- ☐
- ☐
- ☐
- ☐

NOVEMBER
- ☐
- ☐
- ☐
- ☐
- ☐
- ☐
- ☐

DECEMBER
- ☐
- ☐
- ☐
- ☐
- ☐
- ☐
- ☐

Time BLOCKING

WEEK:

	MONDAY	TUESDAY	WEDNESDAY	THURSDAY	FRIDAY	SATURDAY	SUNDAY
5 AM							
6 AM							
7 AM							
8 AM							
9 AM							
10 AM							
11 AM							
12 PM							
1 PM							
2 PM							
3 PM							
4 PM							
5 PM							
6 PM							
7 PM							
8 PM							
9 PM							
10 PM							
11 PM							
12 AM							

Subject CHECKLIST

SEMESTER: _____

SUBJECT ✓   SUBJECT ✓

_____ ☐   _____ ☐
_____ ☐   _____ ☐
_____ ☐   _____ ☐
_____ ☐   _____ ☐
_____ ☐   _____ ☐
_____ ☐   _____ ☐

SUBJECT ✓   SUBJECT ✓

_____ ☐   _____ ☐
_____ ☐   _____ ☐
_____ ☐   _____ ☐
_____ ☐   _____ ☐
_____ ☐   _____ ☐
_____ ☐   _____ ☐

SUBJECT ✓   SUBJECT ✓

_____ ☐   _____ ☐
_____ ☐   _____ ☐
_____ ☐   _____ ☐
_____ ☐   _____ ☐
_____ ☐   _____ ☐
_____ ☐   _____ ☐

237

CPSIA information can be obtained
at www.ICGtesting.com
Printed in the USA
BVHW081341201221
624504BV00006B/715

9 780999 007754